ASIAN BIBLICAL HERMENEUTICS AND POSTCOLONIALISM

The Bible and Liberation

An Orbis Series in Biblical Studies

Norman K. Gottwald and Richard A. Horsley,
General Editors

The Bible & Liberation Series focuses on the emerging range of political, social, and contextual hermeneutics that are changing the face of biblical interpretation today. It brings to light the social struggles behind the biblical texts. At the same time it explores the ways that a "liberated Bible" may offer resources in the contemporary struggle for a more human world.

Already published:

The Bible and Liberation: Political and Social Hermeneutics (revised edition), Norman K. Gottwald and Richard A. Horsley, editors

Josiah's Passover: Sociology and the Liberating Bible, Shigeyuki Nakanose

The Psalms: Songs of Tragedy, Hope, and Justice, J. David Pleins

Women and Jesus in Mark: A Japanese Feminist Perspective, Hisako Kinukawa

Liberating Paul: The Justice of God and the Politics of the Apostle, Neil Elliott

Becoming Children of God: John's Gospel and Radical Discipleship, Wes Howard-Brook

Discovering the Bible in the Non-biblical World, Kwok Pui-lan

Biblical Hermeneutics of Liberation: Modes of Reading the Bible in the South African Context, Gerald West

Apocalypse: A People's Commentary on the Book of Revelation, Pablo Richard

Go Preach! Mark's Kingdom Message and the Black Church Today, Brian K. Blount

Shall We Look for Another? A Feminist Rereading of the Matthean Jesus, Elaine M. Wainwright

The Bible & Liberation Series

ASIAN BIBLICAL HERMENEUTICS AND POSTCOLONIALISM

Contesting the Interpretations

R. S. Sugirtharajah

ORBIS BOOKS
Maryknoll, New York 10545

Grateful acknowledgment is made for permission to reprint the following previously published material:

"Textual Cleansing: From a Colonial to a Postcolonial Version," *Semeia* 76 (1996).

"Orientalism, Ethnonationalism, and Transnationalism: Shifting Identities and Biblical Interpretation," in *Ethnicity and the Bible,* ed. Mark G. Brett (Leiden: E. J. Brill, 1996).

"Jesus in Saffron Robes? The 'Other' Jesus Whom Recent Biographers Forget," *Studies in World Christianity* 1(2) (1995).

The Catholic Foreign Mission Society of America (Maryknoll) recruits and trains people for overseas missionary service. Through Orbis Books, Maryknoll aims to foster the international dialogue that is essential to mission. The books published, however, reflect the opinions of their authors and are not meant to represent the official position of the society.

Published in the United States by Orbis Books, Maryknoll, NY 10545
Manufactured in the United States of America

Library of Congress Cataloging-in-Publication Data

Sugirtharajah, R. S. (Rasiah S.)
    Asian biblical hermeneutics and postcolonialism : contesting the interpretations / R.S. Sugirtharajah.
        p.   cm. – (The Bible & liberation series)
    Includes bibliographical references and index.
    ISBN 1-57075-205-2 (pbk.)
    1. Bible – Hermeneutics. 2. Bible – Criticism, interpretation, etc. – Asia – History. 3. Postcolonialism – Asia. 4. Bible – criticism, interpretation, etc. – India – History.
    5. Postcolonialism – India. I. Title. II. Series.
BS476.S84   1998
220.6'01 – dc21   98-28725

Contents

Acknowledgments   vii

Introduction: Rethinking an Interpretative Agenda   ix

Part I
DISCIPLINING COLONIAL PROJECTS:
TEXTS, COMMENTARIES, AND TRANSLATIONS

1. **From Orientalism to Postcolonialism:**
   Hermeneutics Moving Eastward and Onward   **3**
   The Orientalist Mode: Past Imperfect   4
   The Anglicist Mode: Introduction of Western Tools
       to Shape the Colonial "Other"   8
   The Nativistic Mode: Reinscribing Vernacular Traditions   12
   Toward a Construal of Postcolonial Criticism   15
   Works Cited   25

2. **The Indian Textual Mutiny of 1820: The Brahmin,**
   the Baptist, and Their Contested Interpretations
   of the Bible   **29**
   The Brahmin's Bible   33
   The Heathen and His Hermeneutics   35
   Invader and Invadee and Their Exegetical Enactments   41
   Colonial Clashes   45
   Colonial to Contemporary   50
   Works Cited   52

3. **Imperial Critical Commentaries: Christian Discourse**
   and Commentarial Writings in Colonial India   **54**
   Gentlemen Scholars and Their Hermeneutical Manners   55
   Reframing Christianity   61
   Scripting India   69

Romans, Englishmen, and Indians   75
Concluding Observations   79
Works Cited   84

4. **Textual Cleansing: From a Colonial to a Postcolonial**
   Version   **86**
   Imperial Race, Mercantile Class: Creating the Difference   87
   Effects of the Translations   90
   Toward a Postcolonial Translation Strategy   92
   Works Cited   97

Part II
ORIENTALISM AND BIBLICAL SCHOLARSHIP

5. **Orientalism, Ethnonationalism, and Transnationalism:**
   Shifting Identities and Biblical Interpretation   **101**
   Oriental Mannerisms, Biblical Interpreters   102
   Natives Going Oriental   106
   Natives Deploying Orientalism for Nationalist Ends   107
   Acquiring New Identities   108
   Works Cited   110

6. **Jesus in Saffron Robes? The "Other" Jesus Whom**
   Recent Biographers Forget   **112**
   Hermeneutical Forgetting   113
   Two Traditions as Intertextual Continuum   116
   Locating Hermeneutical Markers for Asia's
      Multifaith Context   117
   Works Cited   119

POSTSCRIPT

7. **Cultures, Texts, Margins: A Hermeneutical Odyssey**   **123**
   Colonial Tools and Hermeneutical Wars   125
   From Colonialism to Orientalism   129
   From Orientalism to Nativism   132
   Searching for a Role: From Nationalism to Postnationality   135
   Works Cited   140

Index   **143**

Acknowledgments

I wish to express my sincere thanks to a number of people who have supported and encouraged me: the staff of Selly Oak Colleges Central Library — Meline Nielson, Susan Abbot, Michael Gale, and Griseleda Lartey — who over the years have become integral to all my research projects and who have become friends more than librarians. I sincerely thank them for their high-caliber service. As the central library now moves into the Orchard Learning Center of the Selly Oak Colleges federation, where the emphasis seems to be high-tech, I have no doubt that Meline, Sue, Michael, and Griseleda will bring warmth, humor, and humanity to the new environment. Thanks also to various students with whom I shared these materials in my "Interpreting the Bible in the Third World" and "Missionary Hermeneutics" classes for their critique and patience; to Dan O'Connor, the unfailing guru, who has given generously of his time, sympathy, and imagination; to Ralph Boradbent for his efficient and caring ways in sorting out my computing problems; to Robert Ellsberg and Sue Perry and other members of Orbis Books for their sensible guidance and enthusiastic support in all our joint projects; to Catherine Costello for her help in the production of this volume; and finally to my wife, Sharada, for her unwavering concern and commitment in all that I do.

R. S. SUGIRTHARAJAH
Selly Oak Colleges
Birmingham, England

Introduction

Rethinking an Interpretative Agenda

Biblical interpreters have often relied on prevailing critical theories to elucidate the Bible. Some current literary theories have been profitably utilized by biblical scholars to look at the Bible's textuality, characterization, plot, and so forth. Social science methods have also been applied to biblical studies. So far, however, there has been relative neglect of one of the most challenging, critical, and controversial theoretical categories of our time — postcolonialism.[1] Surprisingly, despite the massive impact on Asia of imperialism and colonialism, Asian biblical interpretation has managed to insulate itself from the current critical discourse generated by postcolonial critical theory. This volume is a modest attempt to rectify the omission and to mobilize postcolonial concerns as a way of looking at Asian biblical interpretative practices.

The term "postcolonialism" itself is full of complexities and ambivalence, and carries with it a number of issues waiting to be resolved. Particularly, the prefix "post" has caused controversy and hermeneutical confusion. For our purposes, Rey Chow's three specifications — and especially the last one — are relevant. To Chow, the prefix means "having gone through," "after," and "a notion of time which is not linear but constant, marked by events that may be technically finished but that can only be fully understood with the consideration of the devastation they left behind" (1992:152). To clarify further, "postcolonialism" is employed here in a discursive sense of a

---

1. That recent SBL meetings featured postcolonialism indicates that the academy is treating it seriously as a distinctive mode of interpretation. At the 1996 annual meeting in New Orleans two sessions were held on the topic: "Charting Post-colonial Criticism: Deimperializing the Bible and Biblical Interpretation" and "Postcolonialism and Biblical Studies." See *Semeia* 75 (1996) and also *Jian Dao: A Journal of Bible and Theology* 8 (1997) on this theme. Also in the pipeline is the *Postcolonial Bible*, ed. R. S. Sugirtharajah (Sheffield: Sheffield Academic Press, 1998).

resistant discourse which tries to write back and work against colonial assumptions, representations, and ideologies.

The book contains both new and already-published material. The first chapter, "From Orientalism to Postcolonialism: Hermeneutics Moving Eastward and Onward," has had many incarnations as I have worked at clarification. The version that appears here is thoroughly revised, and has substantial new material. This chapter tracks the various modes of interpretation in Asia, and offers postcolonialism as a possible option for the future. One of the significant departures from the earlier versions is to view the Bible itself as problematic and to recognize our need to acknowledge postcolonial unease and ambiguity in relating to it. The Bible is critically interrogated in this chapter for its embodiment of colonial ideas, while its emancipatory potential is recovered by a reading practice informed by a postcolonial perspective, rather than the inherent authority of the Bible.

The next three chapters are freshly written and appear for the first time. The second, "The Indian Textual Mutiny of 1820: The Brahmin, the Baptist, and Their Contested Interpretations of the Bible," looks at the heated polemical battle that ensued when Rammohun Roy, an Indian Hindu, pruned the multiple Gospel attestations about Jesus and produced a single version of the Gospel. Though mission theologians, church historians, and Indologists have looked at this controversy, it has rarely been investigated for the hermeneutical issues it raised for biblical studies and for the importance of the colonial context in which it occurred.

The third chapter, "Imperial Critical Commentaries: Christian Discourse and Commentarial Writings in Colonial India," investigates a series of commentaries, known as the "Indian Church Commentaries," produced during the imperial period in India, and demonstrates how myths of race, nationality, and English superiority were integral to the commentarial strategies and how the commentators' allegiance to the imperial cause informed their biblical exposition.

The fourth chapter, "Textual Cleansing: From a Colonial to a Postcolonial Version," has two parts. The first part investigates the translation strategies and practices of the missionaries during the imperial period, how much of this translating activity was motivated by the class and racial assumptions of the ruler, how this missionary investment in the literary text helped in fixing the colonized culture as stagnant and decadent, and how indigenous texts were seen to be in need of cleansing and purification. The second part of the chapter proposes a different strategy in the changed postcolonial context.

It advocates that, in a religiously plural context like Asia, translation should go beyond the purification of texts to illuminating the Christian texts with the help of local religious texts. It also proposes a postcolonial translation which will mobilize the phenomenal rise of non-native English outside its traditional Anglo-American context, in order to rewrite texts. This chapter was first written as a paper for the National Council of Churches in the United States, for the Bible Translation and Utilization Consultation on the Role of Race and Class in Bible Translation. I am grateful to the participants of the consultation for their incisive comments.

The fifth chapter, "Orientalism, Ethnonationalism, and Transnationalism: Shifting Identities and Biblical Interpretation," seeks to apply the theoretical framework which has come to be associated with Edward Said and goes by the name of "Orientalism." It is a subtle and complex idea of how the West has conceptualized, represented, and codified the knowledge and scholarship about the "Other." Said himself has expressed the hope that further studies will follow his own (1985:24). Cultural critics and practitioners from disciplines such as anthropology and history have taken up Orientalism as an effective tool to investigate their own fields. This chapter is an attempt to apply the elements of Orientalism to biblical studies and to scrutinize both Western and third world biblical scholars for marks of Orientalism in their writings. The article originally appeared in *Ethnicity and the Bible* (ed. Mark Brett [Leiden: E. J. Brill, 1996]) and is reprinted here with some revisions.

Chapter 6, "Jesus in Saffron Robes? The 'Other' Jesus Whom Recent Biographers Forget," looks at one of the great theological revivals of our time — the search for Jesus — and offers a critique from an Asian perspective. Among other things, the chapter aims to unsettle the Eurocentric assumptions underlying the project. An assumption which privileges the Hellenistic and Hebraic background of Jesus' time overlooks the possible influence and impact of Asian religious ideas on the area. This article first appeared in *Studies in World Christianity,* vol. 1, no. 2 (1995).

The last chapter, "Cultures, Texts, Margins: A Hermeneutical Odyssey," narrates, as the subtitle indicates, a hermeneutical journey with which many an Asian biblical interpreter could identify. The key issue the chapter raises is the new phenomenon of the diasporic interpreter, trying to negotiate between the home left behind and the alien milieu. This is a revised version of the plenary lecture given at a special session of "The Bible in Africa, Asia, and Latin America" group, which met at the Society of Biblical Literature Annual Meeting in Chicago in November 1994.

Inevitably, a collection such as this is bound to contain materials which overlap. An advantage is that one need not read the book in the customary linear way, but can enter where convenient. There is, however, an underlying theme which holds the different essays together — namely both critique of and engagement with the Bible and its interpreters.

Such a volume, which is so critical of how one defines and represents the "Other," may trouble readers with passages which are not always sensitive to gender, racial, and religious feeling. Most of the language which we would now regard as insensitive occurs in the passages cited from writings of the colonial era. Instead of cleaning the passages, and cleansing the language of its gender, racial, and religious impurities, they are left as written to indicate how the colonial lexicon codified certain groups, and how the words were employed by both colonizer and colonized, the former as part of the imperial project, the latter unwittingly replicating it. In citing these passages, I have also left untouched the practice of using a capital for "God" and of referring to Jesus with "He," "Him," and "His" as a sign of the reverence these authors felt in such matters.

Readers may also find the use of the disputed and unfashionable term "Third World" offensive. It is used here not in a numerical sense, but as a sociopolitical designation of a people who have been excluded from power and the authority to mold and shape their own lives and destiny. In any event, it is the term the influential group of third world theologians — EATWOT (Ecumenical Association of Third World Theologians) — is happy with and continues to use.

These essays are by no means comprehensive in their application of postcolonial theories to biblical studies and the attendant issues they raise for the discipline. They try to capture a mood which has recently surfaced in biblical interpretation. I hope that these essays provoke further debate and discussion and help to rework the theory and practice of biblical interpretations across divides between Third World and First World, periphery and metropolis.

Works Cited

Chow, Rey. 1992. "Between Colonizers: Hong Kong's Postcolonial Self-Writing in the 1990s." *Diaspora* 2, 2: 151–70.

Said, Edward W. [1978] 1985. *Orientalism.* London: Penguin Books.

Part I

DISCIPLINING COLONIAL PROJECTS

Texts, Commentaries, and Translations

1

From Orientalism to Postcolonialism
Hermeneutics Moving Eastward and Onward

A book of half lives, partial truths, conjecture, interpretation, and perhaps even some mistakes. What better homage to the past than to acknowledge it thus, rescue it and recreate it, without presumption of judgement, and as honestly, though perhaps as incompletely as we know ourselves, as part of the life of which we all are a part? —M. G. VASANJI in *The Book of Secrets*

At the end of it all, I too lie exposed to my own inquiry, also captive to the book. —M. G. VASANJI in *The Book of Secrets*

The intention in this introductory chapter is to work out a possible mode of biblical interpretation for Asia that I will call postcolonial reading or a postcolonial approach. Of course the attempt to establish a postcolonial interpretation will have its application far beyond Asia. Before I explain what postcolonial criticism means, I should like to review briefly various interpretative options now available in Asia.

Unlike the late Pol Pot, no one starts at year zero, or for that matter with a clean slate, and my current research interest is inevitably linked with earlier modes of interpretation. Surveying the Asian scene, I identify three modes of biblical interpretation with origins in the colonial era. These can be categorized as "Orientalist," "Anglicist," and "Nativist." As a future possibility, I would like to propose "Postcolonialist" reading as a mode of interpretation. We will define these modes as we go along. That these categories are yoked to imperialist periodization and couched in colonial terminology is itself a reminder and an indication that the Bible was seen as an ineluctable instrument of the Empire. One of the devices employed to promote the Bible in India was to use King George V's confession that he himself read the Bible every day as propaganda. This enabled missionaries of the time to market the Bible as "the book your Emperor reads" (Roe 1965:153).

The Orientalist Mode: Past Imperfect

Modern biblical interpretation in India began with what is now known as the "Orientalist" phase. Orientalism was the cultural policy advocated by colonialists as a way of promoting and reviving India's ancient linguistic, philosophical, and religious heritage. A generation of Western scholars, known as the Orientalists, initiated a scholarly study of India's ancient sacred, legal, and literary texts. Their interest was instrumental in excavating India's courtly cultural past, and introducing Indians in the process to the accomplishments of their civilization. They also elevated Sanskrit to a venerated status, ensuring that learning the language became important to the natives. Orientalists like William Jones and J. H. Colebrooke saw their task as not only collecting information about Indian textual traditions, customs, and practices, but also making Indians proud custodians of their own history — a history which was capable of rejuvenation, though it had entered a dormant phase through a series of historical accidents. Orientalist policy was instigated partly out of the need to acquaint rulers with the native way of life, and partly as a way of effectively controlling and managing the Indian people.

The Orientalist rejuvenation of Indian culture provided an enormous impetus to the development of biblical interpretation in India. The Indian converts of the nineteenth century, following the path set by their erstwhile Hindu colleagues, were busy retrieving the neglected Indian classical texts rather than engaging with the Western classical tradition as the missionaries had expected. The "natives" were not passive consumers of the past the Orientalists manufactured for them. The indigenous intelligence saw itself as an active interpreter between the past and the present, and busied itself selecting texts and narratives from the past to meet current national concerns. In the writings of Krishna Mohan Banerjea (1813–85), a Bengali convert to Christian faith, one sees an early pioneer. In his book *The Arian Witness*[1] (1875)

---

1. The full title of the book is *The Arian Witness: or the Testimony of Arian Scrip-*

and in his other writings, he demonstrates the remarkable similarities between biblical and Vedic texts. From the great wealth of Vedic writings he selects overlapping narrative segments touching upon the creation, the fall, and the flood, and intertextualizes them with passages from the Christian Scriptures. He saw his task as showing the interconnections between the two textual traditions — Vedic and biblical. His intention was (*a*) to show that the *Vedas* come closer to the spirit of Christianity than do the Hebrew Scriptures; (*b*) to demonstrate that the pristine pure form of Hinduism found in the *Vedas* is identical with the Christian Scriptures; (*c*) to reposition contemporary Indian Christians as spiritual heirs of the Aryan Hindus; and (*d*) to project Vedic Hinduism as a preparation for biblical faith.

> [T]he fundamental principles of the Gospel were recognized, and acknowledged, both in theory and practice, by their primitive ancestors, the Brahmanical Arians of India, and if the authors of the Vedas could by any possibility now return to the world, they would at once recognize the Indian Christians, far more complacently as their own descendants, than any other body of educated natives. (1875:10)

To the annoyance of the missionaries, and to the utter bewilderment of the early Indian converts, Banerjea claimed that the heathen *Vedas* contained hidden mysteries of Christian faith. Banerjea's conclusion was that the *Vedas* anticipated the coming of Christ: "The Vedas shed a peculiar light upon the dispensation of Providence which brought Eastern Sages to worship Christ long before the Westerners had even heard of Him" (Phillip 1982:196).[2] Banerjea's engagement with Vedic texts and biblical narratives was the affirmation, endorsement, and realization of the dream of the Orientalists — that Christian natives would one day encounter native Hindus with their own textual tradition and polemically challenge their own people.

The Orientalist invocation of a lost Golden Age of Indian civilization based on ancient Sanskrit texts and Sanskritic criticism continues to act as a fertile cultural site for Indian Christian biblical interpretation. The hermeneutics of postindependent India developed along a course marked by an excessive use of Sanskritic and brahmanical traditions. Like the earliest Orientalists, some of the current biblical interpreters, including both Indians and expatriates, see the recovery

---

tures in Corroboration of Biblical History and Rudiments of Christian Doctrine. Including Dissertations on the Original Home and Early Adventures of Indo-Arians.

2. See this resource for a selection of Banerjea's writings and an assessment of his theological contribution.

of brahmanical tradition and the reintroduction of Sanskrit as a way of bringing to Indian Christians the truth of their own ancient tradition. The supreme examples of Indian exegetes using ancient Indian texts to elucidate Christian interpretation appear in T. M. Manickam's *Dharma according to Manu and Moses* (1977) and R. H. S. Boyd's *Khristadvaita: A Theology for India* (1977). That Swami Abhishiktananda labeled St. John's Gospel a Christian *Upanishad* (1969:85), in turn inspiring M. A. Amaladoss to reread the same Gospel in the light of the *Upanishads* (1975:7–24), provides another example. Lakshman Wickremesinghe's use of the Markendya story from the Hindu sacred text *Matsya Purana* and various other Hindu myths, and his imaginative juxtaposition of these myths with biblical symbols, falls within the Orientalist phase (1985:4–34).

While these interpreters were encouraging us to engage in comparative hermeneutics, Paul Gregorios (1979), Thomas Manickam again (1982, 1984), Anand Amaladass (1979, 1990, 1994), and Sister Vandana (1989) were making proposals, as an alternative to the hegemonic Western strategies of interpretation, for borrowing critical tools from Sanskritic literary tradition to enhance Indian biblical hermeneutics. Gregorios urged Indians to recover the distinctive interpretative principles laid down by three Indian philosophical schools — the Nyaya, the Vaisesika, and Sankhya — while Manickam proposed a cross-cultural hermeneutics based on three Indian classical schools, Mimamsa, Vyankarana, and the Vedantic school of Sankara, which had developed their own methods to understand revelation. Recently, K. P. Aleaz has suggested the *laksana* method, a method employed by Indian logic for understanding meaning, as a means of exegeting biblical texts (1991:102). The current revival of Sanskritic aesthetical theories — the *dhvani* and *rasa* methods of interpretation — falls within the Orientalist stream.[3] The *dhvani* method has been initiated by Anand Amaladass and Sister Vandana. A ninth-century method of interpretation worked out by Anandavardhana, *dhvani* goes beyond the explicitly stated meaning to the suggestive and evocative nature of texts, and to their hold on the hearer/spectator/reader. It does not dispense with the gains made through the different critical methods such as historical, literary, and rhetorical, but goes beyond them, adding not only the possibility of aesthetic joy in the reading but also a strong commitment to social reconstruction. The *rasa* method

---

3. For utilization of the *dhvani* method in biblical interpretation see *Bible Bhashyam: An Indian Biblical Quarterly* 5, 4 (1979).

recognizes nine distinctive emotional moods that a hearer/spectator/ reader may experience. Basing their work on and at the same time refining the *rasa* method to suit the mood of the psalmists, a German, Martin Kampchen, and an Indian, Jyoti Sahi, look at the Psalms and try to reactivate the reader's emotion, the former through textual comments and the latter through visual presentations (Kampchen and Sahi 1995).

Methodologically, the Sanskritic modes of biblical interpretation which Indian Christians were trying to mobilize varied from the traditional Western modes. Whereas the former tried to construct inner, mystical, and allegorical meaning and transcendent knowledge, the latter tended more toward engaging texts and their textuality, historicity, authorial intentions, and so forth. In Sanskritic exegesis, the text is seen as a medium, marginal to other mediations through which meanings can be obtained.

Orientalistic biblical interpretation functioned at two levels. At a time when missionaries and colonial administrators projected strong negative perceptions of India, an awareness of India's past gained through Oriental scholarship enabled the early Indian converts to invent a patriotic public identity to counter negative assertions. It also enabled later Indian Christians to reexpress Christianity in an Indian form. Wickremesinghe hailed such an enterprise as "Christianity moving Eastwards." The recovery of India's past provided a powerful incentive to admire all things Indian and paved the way for the growth of pan-Indian identity and nationalism. Orientalism provided educated and urbanized Indians a new sense of social and communal identity and encouragement to aspire to a new nationhood. One of the significant contributions of early Orientalism and its subsequent applications was to provide a sense of Indianness, a sense of belonging to a great nation. Unlike the interpretative thrust of the missionaries, which emphasized the saving of individual souls, Indian hermeneutics during the Orientalist phase recast the social identity of the Indian Christian middle class, first in confrontation with the colonial power, and later with the skeptical Hindu majority in postindependent India. Indian Christians were seen by fellow Indians as uprooted and as aliens in their own country. Selecting and legitimating specific elements from the past, and their embrace of ancient Indian values, was a way of renationalizing themselves. Delving into the ancient *Shastras,* Puranas, and *Vedas* was a way of enhancing and rehabilitating their status as authentic Indians.

The Orientalists' attempt to document and discover India resulted in the construction of a particular tradition that equated India with Hindu-Aryan, privileged Sanskrit texts over vernacular, and negated the Indian native and folk traditions. An unchanging, eternally spiritual Hindu India was invented, silencing not only materialistic and theistic lokayata and Sankhya systems, but also Islamic and Persian influences. Orientalists also perpetuated an image of a spiritual India contrasted with a materialist West in a time of rapid social and economic change. The specific form of inequality of gender, the cultural damage done to the tribal peoples, and the psychological damage meted out to the dalits — the untouchables — remained unexamined by Orientalist hermeneutics, though attempts were made to rectify this later.

In summoning a monumentalized, timeless, and spiritual India, Indian interpreters unwittingly contributed to a new form of Orientalism, but this time undertaken by the natives themselves. The natives' need for re-Orientalizing seems in Fanon's words little more than "a banal search for exoticism" (1990:178). To quote him again, the "sari became sacred, and the shoes that come from Paris or Italy are left in favor of pampooties, while suddenly the language of the ruling power is felt to burn your lips" (178). Fanon's caution that the past of Aztec civilization would not affect the present Mexican peasant, or that proof of a wonderful Songhai civilization would not alleviate the plight of the underfed and illiterate Songhai of today, holds equally true for the Indian situation.

The Anglicist Mode: Introduction of Western Tools to Shape the Colonial "Other"

Anglicism arose as an ideological program to counter Orientalism in colonial India. It was a strategic attempt to replace indigenous texts and learning with Western science and Western modes of thinking and to integrate the colonial into the culture of the colonizer. The pioneers among the Anglicists were administrators T. B. Macaulay and Charles Trevelyan, and Alexander Duff, the Church of Scotland's first missionary to India. While the Orientalists marveled at the religious, cultural, and textual heritage of India's past, Anglicists tended to mock it. Macaulay's words aptly sum up the attitude:

[W]e shall countenance, at the public expense, medical doctrines, which would disgrace an English farrier, — Astronomy, which would move laughter in girls at an English boarding school, — History, abounding with kings thirty feet high, and reigns thirty thousand years long, — and Geography, made up of seas of treacle and seas of butter. (Young 1935:351)

Not satisfied with ridiculing Indian learning, the Anglicists identified their advocacy of English literature and European sciences as an endorsement of Christian principles and an advancement of truth, discrediting the Orientalists' reinforcement of Hindu texts as a sign of error. Macaulay writes: "[T]hat literature inculcates the most serious errors on the most important subjects, is a course hardly reconcilable with reason, with morality, ... fruitful of monstrous superstitions, ... false history, false Astronomy, false Medicine, because we find them in company with a false religion" (Young 1935:357). The single aim of the Anglicists was to promote all that was English and Christian. Put differently, while the Orientalists endeavored to turn the Indians into "Vedicmen," the Anglicists tried to mould them into surrogate Englishmen.

Translated into biblical studies, Anglicism meant the introduction of Western modes of biblical investigation in Indian theological colleges. In practice, this meant two things: the importing of Western reading techniques in the form of historical criticism and allied disciplines, and the ushering in of biblical theology with its grand-themes, namely, the Bible as a theologically unified whole, the self-disclosure of God through historical events, the distinctive biblical mentality which differed from the mentality of Hellenistic neighbors, and the unique features of biblical faith in contrast to the Near Eastern environment. Anglicism also brought with it modernist ideas of grand-narratives, modernism's recognition of objective reality, and the view of narratives as objects with determinate meaning; hence, Anglicism brought modernism's commitment to discover *the* single/original meaning of the text. The two biblical commentary series — "Indian Church Commentaries," initiated during the colonial era, and "The Christian Student's Library," developed soon after Indian independence — acted as the vehicles for promoting and validating the Anglicists' intentions. Almost all the commentaries in both series were written by expatriate missionary teachers. These missionary exegetes relied on modernist values for their own empowerment as enlightened educators, but by inculcating these values in their students they helped pave the way at the same time for their cultural and theological enslavement. Elsewhere, and in a later chapter, I have looked at these authors as the cultural products of their time and at the ideology they advanced and legitimized.[4] Here we can simply identify some of the commentaries' main features.

These commentaries painstakingly situate the texts in their historical contexts, and introduce students to the latest European biblical scholarship. The writers were relentless in their aim to propagate the biblical faith as historical and objective, as opposed to the faith of the Hindus, which was seen as mythical and ahistorical. To establish such a claim, the historical-critical method was seen as an appropriate tool and ally. The writers were passionately evangelical in introducing the intricacies of this instrument. Stanley Thoburn hailed it as a divine boon. He wrote in his *Old Testament Introduction,* "The scientific method is one of the greatest gifts that God has given to man, and none can deny the marvellous achievements that have come through its use" (1961:34). The pedagogical use of historical analysis as a method of reading the Bible was the hermeneutical strategy these commentators employed to expose their students to the errors of their own *shastras* and the defects of their philosophical systems, while simultaneously enabling them to internalize the modernist virtues of objective certitude and determinacy. A historical consciousness was seen as necessary for biblical faith. For example, Anthony Hanson wrote:

> [W]e must be willing to have our Bible examined by any reasonable standard of historical criticism, because it is then that the character of Christianity as a religion founded on real historical events will stand out clearly.... On the other hand the events related in the Hindu Scriptures are found to be for the most part legend. (1955:4)

Along with biblical criticism, these volumes, particularly "The Christian Student's Library" series, introduced the chief features of the biblical theology movement that at that time reigned supreme. This movement was shaped by a mosaic of different influences, by Protestant Reformation tradition, the Enlightenment, and the neoorthodoxy of Barth and Brunner, and dealt with European Protestant issues in binary terms of law and grace, justification by faith and justification by works, and the Jesus of history and the Christ of faith. While castigating Indian idol worship as vain and superstitious, biblical theology introduced its own idol in the form of Bultmann's demythologiza-

---

4. For my critique of "Indian Church Commentaries," see chap. 3 in this volume. For a critique of "The Christian Student's Library," see the chapter titled "Biblical Studies in India: From Imperialistic Scholarship to a Postcolonial Mode of Interpretation" in Fernando Segovia and Mary Ann Tolbert, eds., *Teaching the Bible: Discourse on Politics of Biblical Pedagogy* (Maryknoll, N.Y.: Orbis Books, 1998).

tion. Indian readers were encouraged to fall prostrate before this idol, without thinking for a moment that the whole program of demythologization was aimed at Europeans, who had lost the sense of awe and wonder and the feel for the numinous as a result of the scientific mode of thinking. Demythologization was seen as a transferable pedagogic strategy for illuminating the mental darkness of Indians and their superstitious ways.

The Anglicists' project of historical exegesis and biblical theology has been reinforced more recently by M. V. Abraham (1980) and Friedrich Huber (1980). The titles of their papers — "The Teaching of Biblical Theology in India Today" and "Towards an Applicability-Aimed Exegesis" — give us clues to their Anglicist intentions. A quick glance at any issue of the Indian biblical quarterly *Bible Bhashyam* will provide plenty of examples of creative Asian mimicry of Western interpretative methods. Interestingly, these methods are used not only by the hegemonic Asian theologies, but also by a variety of subaltern groups — Indian dalits (Devasahayam 1994, Carr 1994, Gnanavaram 1993, Massey 1994, Maria Arul Raja 1995),[5] Japanese burakumins (Kuribayashi 1995, esp. pp. 101ff.), Korean minjung (Ahn Byung Mu 1985, 1995), indigenous people (Soares-Prabhu 1994a),[6] and Asian women (Kinukawa 1994) — to amplify their voices. Though minjung, dalit, burakumin, and Asian feminist exegesis may look like authentic Korean, Indian, or Japanese products, in a subtle manner they are based on and rework Western reading methods. In other words, methods and theories worked out and originating in Western institutions are used to meet Asian needs. Such an enterprise is not in itself negative. Learning the master's tongue, as Henry Louis Gates has acknowledged, "has been an act of empowerment" (1992:75). We in Asia have been assiduously devoted to learning every new theory which has come out of the Western academy, be it structuralism or narrative criticism, but have drawn upon these modes of interpretative practice to subvert, expose, and liberate both the text and its interpretation. Indians and other Asians have found profitable ways of using the tools of modernity. As the Asian American cultural critic Amy Ling writes, "Tools possess neither memory nor loyalty; they are as effective as the hands wielding them" (1993:741).

---

5. For further examples of dalit hermeneutics see *Jeevadhara: A Journal of Christian Interpretation* 22, 128 (1992).

6. For examples of tribal hermeneutics, see *Jeevadhara: A Journal of Christian Interpretation* 24, 140 (1994).

One of the legacies of the Anglicist mode of interpretation was to help replace the Indian narrative approach with a historical-critical approach. Indians tend to view the texts as authorless narrative wholes and do not show concern for their historicity — their origins or the situations in which they were composed, or the development of their textuality or narrativity — but seek a human story. For Indians the text is only a medium, not a means to understand the truth. It expresses emotive meaning, "feelings, and attitudes rather than . . . ideas, concepts, statements of universal truths, and so forth" (Chari 1993:9). In Indian hermeneutics, the text is valued for its beauty, grace, and emotive power. The interpretative task is not to engage in exegesis but to construct new texts and to retell the stories in a variety of ways. Instead of dissection, recitation, memorization, and repetition are preferred. In introducing historical-critical methods, the Anglicist approach effectively eclipsed indigenous allegorical, symbolic, figurative, and metaphorical reading practices. Indians tend to see narratives as myths with morals, whereas Westerners tend to perceive them as historical constructs with meanings. The narrative approach more recently in vogue in Western biblical circles has tended to vindicate the Indian approach to texts.

The Nativistic Mode:
Reinscribing Vernacular Traditions

Nativistic interpretation arose among those suffocating under the double burden of Western and Sanskritic theories, and who wanted to revive their own language traditions. It is a hermeneutical enterprise which takes place within a specific cultural and language matrix. A good example is what is taking place in Tamil Christianity. P. A. Sathiasatchy, a Tamil Christian poet and lay theologian, endorses the project: "[I]t is high time that, instead of harping on about Indian Christian theology which is prejudiced in favor of Vedic philosophy, we thought in terms of Tamil Christian theology drawn from the context of Tamil culture and its literature and philosophy" (1991:75). He pleads that the time has come for Tamil Christians to search the archives of Tamil literature and legends (1991:82).

Nativism is an attempt to animate *bhasa* or vernacular tradition, prompted by an awareness of the various non-Sanskritic traditions. Significantly, it has helped restore balance by offering an alternative classical culture in Tamil and paving the way for a shift from a vedantic to a bhakti type of religious experience. It has called into question the hegemonic status of Sanskrit and opened up multiple performance and textual traditions. It is a hermeneutical enterprise bound by the rules set by a particular language and culture.

The nativistic biblical interpretations of Sadhu Sundar Singh (Punjabi), Mungamuri Devadas (Telugu), Vaman Tilak (Marathi), and H. A. Krishna Pillai (Tamil) borrow largely from the vernacular mode of storytelling. Traditionally, narrative was seen as the dominant medium and the most compelling vehicle for moral instruction, religious teaching, and doctrinal explication. Sadhu Sundar Singh's method of biblical exposition puts him firmly within the Indian religious storytellers' tradition. In his rendition of biblical stories, the Sadhu not only minutely dissects the text, but also draws on ancient and contemporary Indian tales, retelling them and connecting them both with lived experience and with the Christian Scriptures. Even a cursory glance at his writings will indicate how often his biblical exposition is sprinkled with tales, anecdotes, and aphorisms (Francis 1993). Likewise, Vaman Tilak's attempt to write a life of Jesus in Marathi verse — as a great Christian purana, *Christayan* — was comparable with and based on the great Hindu epic the *Ramayana* (Winslow 1923:105f.) Iyadurai Bhagavatar, a Tamil Catholic, drew on the *kaletchepam* method to expound biblical stories. This was a method devised by Hindu pundits as an imaginative way of teaching the intricacies of the *Vedas* to ordinary people through musical accompaniments and recitations (Immanuel 1950:137–39). This tradition is now carried on in what Thangaraj calls "singable theology" (1990:109–18).

Nativism borrows vocabulary as well as concepts from bhakti, the devotional writings, and recasts them to describe biblical ideas. The works of H. A. Krishna Pillai, G. S. Vedanayagam Sastriar, and A. J. Appasamy fall within this category. While Krishna Pillai and Vedanayagam used the Tamil poetic tradition to renarrate the Christian story, Appasamy drew on bhakti insights to reread biblical texts. His exegetical work on John's Gospel appeared in two volumes, *Christianity as Bhakti Marga* ([1926] 1991) and *What Is Moksa?* (1931). For generations of Indian Christians, Appasamy has been responsible for popularizing John as a mystical, spiritual Gospel. In his reading of John 10:30, "I and the father are one," he came up with an interesting exegetical suggestion. He contested both the traditional Chalcedonian understanding of the union between the father and the son as metaphysical and also the Hindu monistic tendency to view the union in the advaitic (nondual) sense. Utilizing instead the bhakti type of visis-

tadvaita (modified nonduality) of Ramanuja, he refigured the union as
moral and functional (1942:35–39). Jaswant Raj's intertextual study
of grace in the writings of Paul and the *Thiruvarutpayan* (The Gain
of Divine Grace), the twelve books of the hymns of the Tamil Saivite
saints (1989), and a similar comparative attempt by Corona Mary to
look at the Johannine understanding of birth in the spirit alongside another Saiva text, *Meikanda Sastram* (1995), fall within this category
of nativistic interpretation.

A striking feature of nativism is its apologetic tone. Since most
of the bhasa-tradition writers were recent converts, they were well
qualified to expose the defects of the religion they had left behind.
Krishna Pillai's *Ratchanya Camaya Nirnayam* (The determination of
the religion of salvation) (1898) is an illustration.

Native hermeneutics promoted an awareness of often neglected indigenous traditions. It compensated for the regrettable Orientalist and
Anglicist neglect of non-Sanskritic and vernacular literary forms, empowering Christian interpreters to work within their own language and
providing a rich field of metaphors. In the process, native hermeneutics
enabled interpreters to address audiences in a common language.

The problem with nativistic interpretation is its particularism and
isolationism. It is culture-bound, and hence always in danger of being
ghettoized and becoming irrelevant to the majority outside its region.
Due to the assumption that it is uncontaminated by external influence,
it is accorded privileged status. We need to ask again, however, in an
emerging complex of global interconnections whether we can still talk
of a pure culture not infected by globalization. In addition, nativistic interpretation perpetuates the notion of local culture as static and
unchanging, and tends to idealize it. Portraying people as confined
to one locality is very much an illusion. Arjun Appadurai, the social
anthropologist, reminds us that groups "confined to and by places to
which they belong,...unsullied by contact with a larger world, have
probably never existed" (1988:39). For instance, Krishna Pillai's mag-
num opus, *Ratchanya Yathrikam,* celebrated for its use of the Tamil
poetic tradition, is in fact based on John Bunyan's *The Pilgrim's
Progress.*

At the risk of oversimplification, I have outlined here three interpretative models that are currently available. It is important to recognize
that these do not supersede one another, but often overlap and coexist.
More important, they continue to provide hermeneutical impulses to
countless interpreters.

Toward a Construal of Postcolonial Criticism

Two critical categories at the center of current hermeneutical discussion are *postmodernism* and *postcolonialism*. Needless to say, much controversy surrounds the status and value of these discourses. Nonetheless, they have certain affinities. Both are clearly products of discomfort over modernistic thinking, which fostered an excessive reverence for reason, a spurious belief in objective truth, savage control over the environment, and less-critical respect for such institutions as the nation-state. More important, both are offshoots of the crumbling of Western political and cultural hegemony and its imperialistic tendencies. Sadly, it is here that the alliance ends. Postmodernism is still seen as Eurocentric in its conceptual and aesthetic thrust. It is found wanting from a third world perspective on several fronts: its lack of a theory of resistance; its failure to cultivate a transformative agenda due to its detached attitudes; its revalidation of the local and its celebration of differences, which are liable to lead to further alienation of subalterns thus assigned to their own space and concerns; its repudiation of and skepticism toward grand-narratives, which fail to take into account liberation as an emancipatory metastory and as a potent symbol for those whose rights have been negated, circumvented, or put in abeyance. Though attempts are made to collapse postmodernism and postcolonialism into one and to erase their differences, postcolonialism is emerging as a distinctive discourse. Evidence comes with the recognition of postcolonialism as a branch of cultural studies and the rapid emergence of a supporting literature (Williams and Chrisman 1993; Ashcroft, Griffiths, and Tiffin 1995; Mongia 1996; Childs and Williams 1997; and Moore-Gilbert 1997).

"Postcolonialism" is a contentious term. The question of its usefulness and validity has provoked a vigorous debate among people at different institutions.[7] Considering its relatively recent entry into the Western academy, it has successfully brought to the hermeneutical agenda the overlapping issues of race, empire, diaspora, and ethnicity. It must be stressed that it is not a homogenous project, but a hermeneutical salmagundi, consisting of extremely varied methods, materials, historical entanglements, geographical locations, political affiliations, cultural identities, and economic predicaments. The current emergence of postcolonial discourse does not in any way overshadow the vigorous

---

7. For a searching and skeptical critique, see Ahmad (1992), Shohat (1992), McClintock (1992), Miyoshi (1993), Dirlik (1994), and Trivedi and Mukherjee (1996). For a discussion of challenges to postcolonial criticism from within and outside the field, see Moore-Gilbert (1997), 11–22.

interrogations which went on during the halcyon days of colonialism, spearheaded by nationalists and later by Marxist theoreticians. The difference is that the earlier interventions utilized the master narratives, which not only originated in the West but also effectively put the West at the center. The current postcolonial criticism takes the critique of Eurocentrism as its central task. The debate centers around, among other things, whether Eurocentrism concerns a state, a condition, or a critical reading strategy. Negatively put, postcolonialism is not about historical stages or periodization. Neither is it about lowering the flags of empire and wrapping oneself with new national flags. Positively, it signifies three things — representation, identity, and a reading posture, emerging among the former victims of colonialism.

Postcoloniality involves the once-colonized "Others" insisting on taking their place as historical subjects. Unlike other current theoretical practices such as feminism and structuralism, postcolonial discourse is not about the West, but about the colonized "Other." Those once assigned to the mofussil appear at metropolitan centers as confident, indomitable, and indispensable partners in the dialogue and collaborate with the dispossessed and disadvantaged in the West. Gyan Prakash sums up the new situation:

> The third world, far from being confined to its assigned space, has penetrated the inner sanctum of the first world in the process of being "third worlded" — arousing, inciting, and affiliating with the subordinated others in the first world. It has reached across boundaries and barriers to connect with the minority voices in the first world: socialists, radicals, feminists, minorities. (1990:403)

The arrival of the once colonized indicates that it is not business as usual in the metropolis. The prohibitive Orient-Occident boundaries are lowered and crossed, creating an engagement which will release the Third World from its marginal status.

Second, linked to the above, postcoloniality is about acquiring a new identity. One of the legacies of colonialism is an intermingling of people and cultures, and the result is a hybridized identity — the formation of hyphenated, fractured, multiple, and multiplying identities. Previously such attempts by the "natives" to redraw their identity by fusing indigenous and imported values was labeled syncretism and dismissed as a disruptive and negative project. Such criticism was grounded in Western Christian exclusivity and expansionist perspectives. Hybridity, however, is a wider and more complex web of cultural negotiation and interaction, forged by imaginatively redeploying the local and the imported elements. It is not about the melting away of the difference between "us" and "them," or East and West, or about dislodging the colonial construct of the "Other," but involves a newfound independence, achieved not simply by rejecting provincial, national, and imperial attachments, but by working through them (see Said 1993:407). Appellations like Indian, dalit, and Tamil may be convenient starting points, but these identities are constantly and consistently undergoing change. The distinguishing feature of the new identity will be that it will go beyond the categories and representations worked out by Orientalists, Anglicists, and nativists, who tend to work with core elements such as nationality, spirituality, ethnicity, caste, femininity, and so forth, and will imaginatively forge a complex set of new identities that juggle different values and concepts.

Third, postcoloniality is a critical enterprise aimed at unmasking the link between ideas and power which lies behind Western texts, theories, and learning. Postcolonial discourse is not about the territorial ejection of imperial powers or about learning, Caliban-like, the art of cursing the evils of empire. Rather, it is an active interrogation of the hegemonic systems of thought, textual codes, and symbolic practices which the West constructed in its domination of colonial subjects. In other words, postcolonialism is concerned with the question of cultural and discursive domination. It is a discursive resistance to imperialism, imperial ideologies, and imperial attitudes and to their continual reincarnations in such wide fields as politics, economics, history, and theological and biblical studies. Resistance is not simply a reaction to colonial practices, but an alternative way of perceiving and restructuring society.

I imagine that postcoloniality will be the arena in which future biblical interpretation in India, and in Asia for that matter, will be worked out. The interpretation will emerge from people who once were colonized by European powers — or, in the case of Korea, by imperial Japan — but who now have some political freedom, while continuing to live with burdens from the past and experiencing forms of economic and cultural neocolonialism. The interpretation will emerge from the economic, social, and cultural margins, which will be seen as "sites of survival," "fighting grounds," and "sites for pilgrimage" (Trinh 1991:17). It will emerge among nations, communities, and groups which have been victims of the old imperialism and are now victims of the current globalization, and who have been kept away from power only to achieve an identity nurtured and nourished by their own goals and aspirations.

Postcolonial interpretation will be a way of critiquing both the Bible and the universalist, totalizing forms of European interpretation that were passed on to us. It will interrogate biblical narratives with the same ideological and theoretical questions which are put to other texts. Its pages will be searched for embedded colonial ideology and practice and will be scrutinized for constructions of conquest and settlement, colonial relations, and the concomitant questions arising in the wake of colonialism, such as the place of the colonized subjects, deportation, asylum, assimilation, deterritorialization, and so forth. This mode of interpretation will engage theoretically with the central question of the Bible's promotion of xenophobic, expansionist, militaristic, and ethnic tendencies. Unlike the Orientalist, Anglicist, and nativist modes, it will not engage in recovering *the* single meaning of the text, but will probe the text for its implicit or explicit colonial codes. The retrieval and reinscription of the past becomes a crucial hermeneutical activity. Unlike the Orientalist, Anglicist, and nativist approaches, however, postcolonial reading will negotiate the past, "not as a static fetishized phase to be literally reproduced, but as fragmented sets of narrated memories and experiences on the basis of which to mobilize contemporary communities" (Shohat 1992:109).

What will distinguish postcolonial reading from Orientalist and Anglicist modes of interpretation is the conviction that the modernist values these earlier modes espoused, such as objectivity and neutrality, are expressions of political, religious, and scholarly power. Postcolonial interpretation will reject the myth of objective or neutral truth and will replace it with a perception of truth as mapped, constructed, and negotiated. Postcolonial criticism recognizes that interpreters have to be freed from traditional interpretative powers so that the voice of the voiceless may be heard. Such freedom will be manifest in what Fanon calls "fighting literature," "a revolutionary literature" (1990:179), the authentic expression of people tired of the exasperating attempts to assimilate and mimic the hegemonic Orientalist and Anglicist modes of interpretation. It will revalorize the hidden or occluded accounts of numerous groups — women, minorities, the disadvantaged, and the displaced.

The Bible and Its Imperial Content

Twin interpretative tasks attach themselves to postcolonial biblical criticism. One is to interrogate the biblical narratives and the interpretations which legitimize and reinscribe colonial interests. The other is to engage in an emancipatory reading of the texts, informed by a hermeneutic yoked to postcolonial concerns. The interest of postcolonial criticism does not lie in the truth of the text but in the central question of its promotion of colonial ideology. The text is studied not for its own sake, or even for the theological and spiritual direction and inspiration it may be thought to provide, but for those intrinsic textual features which embody colonial codes. While exposing the colonial components and compromises in the biblical narratives, postcolonial biblical criticism will also seek to rehabilitate those narratives relevant to a reading practice shaped by interlocking postcolonial concerns such as migration, self-determination, ethnicity, and so forth.

Postcoloniality brings a fresh set of questions to the Bible. The Bible as the book of the colonizer is well attested and documented in mission history. But those who take postcoloniality seriously will go a step further and, instead of assigning blame to the missionary interpreters, will perceive the Bible itself as a literary product of the ancient world, both embodying and legitimizing colonial intentions, assumptions, and power, and also reflecting the predicament of a frequent victim of its neighbors' imperial and colonial intentions. As a land sitting on a corridor joining the land masses of Europe, Asia, and Africa, it could hardly have been otherwise. Most of the Bible's writings are thus set in an imperial context and are made to serve the militaristic, expansionist impulses of Israel and to respond to those of Egypt, Assyria, Persia, and Rome. Those substantial parts of biblical narrative emerging in such contexts treat the questions which arise in the wake of colonialism, such as nationalism, ethnicity, deterritorialization, multiple identities, and citizenship. In other words, colonialism dominates and determines the interest of the biblical texts, and we could reasonably describe the Bible as a colonial document, though confessional and faith language often overlays and ignores the interconnecting postcolonial questions.

Postcolonial biblical criticism will look for textual indicators which underscore colonial ideologies and investigate these texts for collusion with the establishment. The book of Esther provides a case in point. It is a colonial story in which the colonized, Esther, as Itumeleng Mosala has demonstrated, does not challenge the assumptions of the dominant Persian empire, but, instead, strives for a mode of survival or at best some degree of influence within that system (1992). In Mosala's deconstruction, the narrative promotes a survivalist agenda which is not supported by any emancipatory praxis. It advocates incorporation and assimilation. Utilizing these strategies, Esther is eventually received into the royal household, and Mordecai receives an appointment in the colonial administration. Such narrative has only a monitory relevance for those in current diasporic communities seeking to negotiate an identity and a role in an alien context. A strategy of assimilation encourages conformity to the values and behavior of the dominant society, and assumes that these values are static and good for all.

The two important figures in the New Testament who have experienced colonialism, Jesus and Paul, have little to say on its impact and effect. Jesus' ministry is set in the political context of Roman imperialism, but there is hardly any evidence of his direct critique of the Roman Empire or the Herodian kingship. His attack is reserved for locals who collude with the Romans and make effective use of the Temple system to advance their cause. Paul, a genuine immigrant by current political standards, gives the impression in his writings that he has been fully co-opted into the imperial system. An example occurs in Romans 13, in which he reinscribes colonial values by asserting that God and history are on the side of the Roman Empire. The sensible thing for Christians, Paul writes, is to live peaceably with the colonial administration and to work within its framework, rather than to revolt. The almighty Roman power was hardly questioned in his epistles, except in teleological terms. Occasionally he censures the evils of the Empire, but offers no political strategy or practical solution for its liquidation. The other letters addressed to Christians living in the Roman-occupied regions, such as Asia Minor or Crete, recapitulate the Pauline advice (1 Pet. 2:13–14; Titus 3:1). The writer of the letter to Colossians encapsulates the mood: "[F]or in him all things were created, in heaven and on earth, visible and invisible, whether thrones or dominions or principalities or authorities — all things were created through him, and for him" (1:16). The prescription these documents offer to their readers is simply to endure in their belief in the return of Jesus, who will bring liberation to the tyrannized world.

Marks of Postcolonial Scriptural Reading

While recognizing the importance of recovering the past, postcolonial criticism remains cognizant of the difficulty in using ancient texts. The Bible is an ideologically loaded text and never a neutral container. Reading the Bible from a postcolonial perspective implies removing the colonial assumptions and ideologies on which much of the text rests. Postcolonial interrogation makes clear that though, confessionally, we may have no qualms about admitting the Bible's relevance to our immediate context, the biblical narrative in some ways is not about us. Yet we return to its narratives, in a place and time utterly different from the milieu from which the biblical materials emerged. Postcolonial criticism does not stop with questions about the nature and status of the texts, but has another fundamental hermeneutical task — what to do with them? Such reading is compelled to focus on the concerns of postcoloniality in the construal of meaning.

There are several marks of postcolonial criticism. One is identified by cultural critic Stuart Hall when he advocates looking in the text for what he calls oppositional or protest voices. He identifies four codes embodied in current discourse on television — hegemonic, professional, negotiated, and protest or oppositional (Hall 1973:16–19). Biblical texts reflect all four codes; traditional interpretations generally fraternize with the first three. Postcolonialism, in contrast, will look for protesting or oppositional voices, for instance, in the parable of the tenants (Mark 12:1–11, Matt. 21:33–43, and Luke 20:9–18). Commentators often invest this parable with allegorical meanings or look for allusions to the Hebrew Bible. It is usually read either from an overly christological or from the property owner's perspective. In the Church of England, for example, this parable was for many years a set reading for January 30, the day Charles I was beheaded. The notation in the rubric, "King and Martyr," indicates how those who wielded power appropriated the parable to reinscribe the point of view of the establishment. Rarely is the parable read from the point of view of the people in the audience. Most commentators ignore their role. When one by one the tenants kill the messengers, the householder finally sends his son, who is also killed. What will the owner do? asks Jesus, and goes on to say that he will destroy those tenants and give the vineyard to others. This parable occurs in Mark, Matthew, and Luke, but in Luke, unlike the other two accounts, the parable is specifically told to the people, who have an interesting reaction. Hearing that the owner is going to destroy the tenants and give the land to others, the people's response is "God forbid" (Luke 20:16b). They express shock, for they are the heirs of Yahweh's allotment of land, which has been stolen from them. The audience knows that once the land is lost they not only will lose the income but will be at the mercy of the new owner's working arrangements.

Another example of the protest voice is the often overlooked, enigmatic saying of the blind man at Bethsaida (Mark 8:24). While he was getting his sight back, Jesus asked: "Do you see anything?" His literal reply, according to the difficult reading that many preferred, was: "I see men for [or that] like trees I see them walking." Western biblical commentators have attempted to make sense of this puzzling statement in a number of ways.[8] Some attribute the awkwardness of the saying to Mark's misreading of an ambiguous Aramaic word, or skirt around the illogic by resorting to a freer paraphrase. Some question the genuineness of the man's blindness, or discover symbolism in the healing act. Such readings have their origins in the imposition by Western commentators of universalism, personal pietism, or both on the Markan text.[9] But once Mark is located in the imperial context, and his writing is seen as the voice of a subjugated people in opposition to imperial order and its institutions, one sees a different — a subversive — meaning in the statement. A clue to solve the puzzling vision of walking trees may be found in the book of Judges, which records a reference to trees walking in a fable Jotham tells about trees going about to elect their king (9:7–15). Jotham's fable satirizes the kingship of Abimelech over the lords of Shechem. As the trees go about choosing a king, none of the fruit trees approached — olive, fig, or vine — wants to give up its purposeful existence, so the crown goes to the bramble. The point of the fable is that the institution of kingship is utterly useless, just as a bramble is useless as a source of shade; it is also a lethal institution, just as brambles are a potent source of forest fire. Even without going into historical details, the purpose of the fable is clear. It offers a severe criticism of those who aspire to empire and domination. The blind man's vision is a graphic protestation against imperial order and alien rule, and those who collaborate with it.

Postcolonial criticism brings such marginal elements to the front and, in the process, subverts the traditional meaning. It engages in archival exegesis as a way of rememorializing the narratives and voices which have been subjected to institutional and exegetical forgetting.

The second mark of postcolonial reading is that it will not romanticize or idealize the poor. When treating the widow's offering (Mark 12:41–44, Luke 21:1–4), hegemonic readings tend to valorize the poor. The widow is often portrayed as a prime example of Christian discipleship, piety, and sacrifice: "[T]he devotion and self-sacrifice of the poor widow stand out against the dark background of the

---

8. For various exegetical positions see R. S. Sugirtharajah, "Men, Trees, and Walking: A Conjectural Solution to Mk. 8:24," *The Expository Times* 103, 6 (1992): 172–74.

9. For a postcolonial reading of Mark's Gospel, see Richard A. Horsley, "Submerged Biblical Histories and Imperial Biblical Studies," in *The Postcolonial Bible,* ed. R. S. Sugirtharajah (Sheffield: Sheffield Academic Press, forthcoming).

self-indulgence and false piety of the scribes and the easy and ostentatious giving of the rich" (Witherington 1987:18). At times she is seen as a model for Christian giving (Hargreaves 1975:214; Stegemann 1984:63–64). The trouble with the first reading is that there is no record of the widow ever becoming an admirer of Jesus or joining one of the numerous groups of women who followed him. The difficulty with the second reading is that it fails to take note of the ultimate destination of the money. It also overlooks what Jesus thought of the Temple and the role it played in the life of the Jews. At least eight alleged sayings of Jesus predict the destruction of the Temple; at his trial this prediction is brought up as a charge. What is significant about the narrative of the widow's offering is that Mark and Luke juxtapose the incident between two scenes. In the first, Jesus castigates the devouring of the property of widows; in the second, Jesus, at the treasury, predicts the destruction of the Temple. Viewed in this way, the widow is not singled out by Jesus "as a model for appropriate *action!*" (Malbon 1994:78; italics in the original), but as a woman manipulated and conned by the system into parting with what little she had.

The third mark of postcolonial reading is that, unlike the dominant reading, it will not blame the victims, but will direct attention to the social structures and institutions which spawn victimhood. For instance, when reading the Johannine account of the woman caught in adultery (7:53–8:11), it will not apportion blame to the woman, as the traditional patriarchal and puritanical readings tend to do, but will focus on Jesus' critique of the system codified by the cultural norms and perpetuated by the social order and its guardians. It will focus on the failure of the pollution and purity system as an avenue for liberation.

The other mark of postcolonial reading will be its advocacy of a wider hermeneutical agenda to place the study of sacred texts — Christian-Hindu, Christian-Buddhist, Christian-Confucian — within the intersecting histories which constitute them. It will replace the totalitarian and totalizing claims of biblical narratives with the claim that they have to be understood as the negotiated narrative strategies of a community, to be read and heard along with other communally inspired sacred narratives. A postcolonial reading will see these texts within an intertextual continuum, embodying a multiplicity of perspectives. This will mean looking for the hermeneutical relations that these texts imply and inspire, and will resist any attempts to subsume one relationship under the other. The issue is how these diverse texts can help us account for our collective identities. The recent study of Matthew's missionary command, which George Soares-Prabhu read alongside the Buddhist *Mahavagga* text, comes close to the postcolonial intertextual engagement I have in mind (Soares-Prabhu 1994b). The Other is celebrated in his article without insisting on the protocols set by missionary apologetic and fitting into them. He has demonstrated how such a wider intertextual reading will begin to "reveal the biblical way to the 'disinterested action' (*nishkama karma*) of the Bhagavadgita (2.47; 4.18–20), or to that unshakable 'calm' (*santam*), like that of a deep lake clear and still, which in the Dhammapada (6.7; 7.7) is the mark of the 'saint' (*arhant*)" (1994b:273). Such an interactive reading will help to arrive at a fuller interpretation of various religious texts.

The above examples are by no means comprehensive, but illustrate the reworking involved in postcolonial biblical criticism. In the future, postcolonial criticism will interrogate the underlying assumptions which privilege literary over oral narratives.

Finally, theories, however neat or sophisticated, have the potential themselves to become colonialist. While they may have an inherent ability to resist, expose, and shift the mood of a discourse, they also have totalizing tendencies, are prone to oppress other subalterns, and, far worse, to end up as incomprehensible and inaccessible, and to flummox the very people they are intended to help. Ultimately, at stake is not whether postcolonial discourse has helped change the terms of the master discourse or helped its practitioners win a place at the master's table. The point is that decolonization does not start with the deconstruction of the text, or with an approving nod from metropolitan practitioners. Textual reclamations and resistant exegetical practices will make sense only if they address the questions people face today. At a time when people are thrown together and live in multilingual, multiracial, and multifaith societies, the question is how a people can affirm their language, take pride in their race, be fervent about their faith, cherish their ethnicity, and celebrate their differences and at the same time share the land, its water, and its fruits with others who also make claims about their language, ethnicity, religion, and culture. The task before us is not so much to celebrate the new hybridized identity or to marvel at the way we have used the right jargon as a posture and power play, but to help in addressing the questions which affect people's lives. The worth and the credibility of postcolonial criticism will be judged by how it orchestrates the unique and fragile and imagined claims of one community against another.

Works Cited

Abhishiktananda, Swami. 1969. *Hindu-Christian Meeting Point: Within the Cave of the Heart.* Bombay: Institute of Indian Culture.

Abraham, M. V. 1980. "The Teaching of Biblical Theology in India Today." *The Indian Journal of Theology* 29:124–32.

Ahmad, Aijaz. 1992. In *Theory: Classes, Nations, Literatures.* London: Verso.

Ahn Byung Mu. 1985. "The Body of Jesus-Event Tradition." *East Asia Journal of Theology* 3, 2:293–309.

———. 1995. "Jesus and the Minjung in the Gospel of Mark." In *Voices from the Margin: Interpreting the Bible in the Third World.* New edition. Ed. R. S. Sugirtharajah. Maryknoll, N.Y.: Orbis Books, pp. 85–104.

Aleaz, K. P. 1991. *The Role of Pramanas in Hindu-Christian Epistemology.* Calcutta: Punthi-Pustak.

Amaladass, Anand. 1979. " 'Dhvani' Theory in Sanskrit Poetics." *Bible Bhashyam: An Indian Biblical Quarterly* 5, 4:261–75.

———. 1990. "Dhvani Theory and Interpretation of Scripture." *The Adyar Library Bulletin* 54:68-98.

———. 1994. "Dhvani Method of Interpretation and Biblical Hermeneutics." *Indian Theological Studies* 31, 3:199–217.

Amaladoss, M. A. 1975. "An Indian Reads St. John's Gospel." In *India's Search for Reality and the Relevance of the Gospel of John.* Ed. Christopher Duraisingh and Cecil Hargreaves. Delhi: ISPCK, pp. 7–21.

Appadurai, Arjun. 1988. "Putting Hierarchy in Its Place." *Cultural Anthropology* 3, 1:36–49.

Appasamy, A. J. [1926] 1991. *Christianity as Bhakti Marga: A Study of the Johannine Doctrine of Love.* Madras: Christian Literature Society.

———. 1931. *What Is Moksa? A Study in the Johannine Doctrine of Life.* Madras: Christian Literature Society.

———. 1942. *The Gospel and India's Heritage.* London: SPCK.

Ashcroft, Bill, Gareth Griffiths, and Helen Tiffin, eds. 1995. *The Postcolonial Studies Reader.* London: Routledge.

Banerjea, K. M. 1875. *The Arian Witness: or the Testimony of Arian Scriptures in Corroboration of Biblical History and Rudiments of Christian Doctrine. Including Dissertations on the Original Home and Early Adventures of Indo-Arians.* London: Thacker, Spink & Co.

Boyd, Robin H. S. 1977. *Khristadvaita: A Theology for India.* Madras: Christian Literature Society.

Carr, Dhyanchand. 1994. "A Biblical Basis for Dalit Theology." In *Indigenous People: Dalits. Dalit Issues in Today's Theological Debate.* Ed. James Massey. Delhi: ISPCK, 231–49.

Chari, V. K. 1993. *Sanskrit Criticism.* Delhi: Motilal Banarsidass Publishers.

Childs, Peter, and Patrick R. J. Williams. 1997. *An Introduction to Postcolonial Theory.* London: Prentice Hall.

Devasahayam, V. [1992] 1994. *Outside the Camp: Biblical Studies in Dalit Perspective.* Madras: Department of Research and Publications, Gurukul Lutheran Theological College and Research Institute.

Dirlik, Arif. 1994. "The Postcolonial Aura: Third World Criticism in the Age of Global Capitalism." *Critical Inquiry* 20, 2:328–56.

Fanon, Frantz. [1961] 1990. *The Wretched of the Earth.* Harmondsworth: Penguin Books.

Francis, Dayanandan T., ed. [1989] 1993. *The Christian Witness of Sadhu Sundar Singh: A Collection of His Writings.* Madras: Christian Literature Society.

Gates, Henry Louis. 1992. *Loose Canons: Notes on the Culture Wars.* New York: Oxford University Press.

Gnanavaram, M. 1993. " 'Dalit Theology' and the Parable of the Good Samaritan." *Journal for the Study of the New Testament* 50:59-83.

Gregorios, Paul. 1979. "Hermeneutics in India Today in the Light of World Debate." *Indian Journal of Theology* 28, 1:1–14. Reprinted in *Readings in Indian Christian Theology.* Vol. 1. Ed. R. S. Sugirtharajah and Cecil Hargreaves. London: SPCK, 1993, pp. 176–85.

Hall, Stuart. 1973. *Encoding and Decoding in the Television Discourse.* Birmingham, England: Center for Cultural Studies.

Hanson, Anthony. 1955. *Jonah and Daniel: Introduction and Commentary.* The Christian Students' Library 9. Madras: Christian Literature Society.

Hargreaves, John. 1975. *A Guide to St. Mark's Gospel.* TEF Study Guide 2. London: SPCK.

Huber, Friedrich. 1980. "Towards an Applicability-Aimed Exegesis." *Indian Journal of Theology* 29:133–48.

Immanuel, Rajappan D. 1950. *The Influence of Hinduism on Indian Christians.* Jabalpur: Leonard Theological College.

Jaswant Raj, Joseph. 1989. *Grace in the Saiva Siddhantham and in St. Paul: A Contribution in Inter-faith Cross-cultural Understanding.* Madras: South Indian Salesian Society.

Kampchen, Martin, and Jyoti Sahi. 1995. *The Holy Waters: Indian Psalm Meditations.* Bangalore: Asian Trading Corporation.

Kinukawa, Hisako. 1994. *Women and Jesus in Mark: A Japanese Feminist Perspective.* Maryknoll, N.Y.: Orbis Books.

Krishna Pillai, H. A. 1898. *Ratchanya Camaya Nirnayam* (The determination of the religion of salvation). Sivakasi: Chandra Printers. [In Tamil.]

Kuribayashi, Teruo. 1995. "The Story of the Buraku People of Japan." In *God, Christ, and God's People in Asia.* Ed. Dhyanchand Carr. Hong Kong: CCA Theological Concerns, pp. 90–114.

Ling, Amy. 1993. "I'm Here." In *Feminism: An Anthology of Literature Theory and Criticism.* Ed. Robyn R. Warhol and Diane Price Herndl. New Brunswick, N.J.: Rutgers University Press, pp. 738–45.

Manickam, T. M. 1977. *Dharma according to Manu and Moses.* Bangalore: Dharmaram Publications.

————. 1982. "Towards an Indian Hermeneutics of the Bible." *Jeevadhara: A Journal of Christian Interpretation* 12, 68:94–104.

————. 1984. "Cross Cultural Hermeneutics: The Patterns of Jaimini, Bhartrhari, and Sankaracharya." *Indian Theological Studies* 21, 3–4:250–67.

Malbon, Elizabeth Struthers. 1994. "The Major Importance of the Minor Characters in Mark." In *The New Literary Criticism and the New Testament*. Ed. Edgar V. McKnight and Elizabeth Struthers Malbon. Valley Forge, Pa.: Trinity Press International, pp. 58–86.

Maria Arul Raja, A. 1995. "The Authority of Jesus: A Dalit Reading of Mark 11.27–33." *Jeevadhara: A Journal of Christian Interpretation* 25, 146:123–38.

Mary, Corona. 1995. "Divinisation through Grace: Understanding a Johannine Theme in the Light of Saiva-Sidhanta." *Jeevadhara: A Journal of Christian Interpretation* 25, 146:161–72.

Massey, James. 1994. *Towards Dalit Hermeneutics: Re-reading the Text, the History, and the Literature*. Delhi: ISPCK.

McClintock, Anne. 1992. "The Angel of Progress: Pitfalls of the Term 'Postcolonialism.'" *Social Text* 31, 32:84–98.

Miyoshi, Masao. 1993. "A Borderless World? From Colonialism to Transnationalism and the Decline of the Nation-State." *Critical Inquiry* 19:726–51.

Mongia, Padmini. 1996. *Contemporary Postcolonial Theory: A Reader*. London: Arnold.

Moore-Gilbert, Bart. 1997. *Postcolonial Theory: Contexts, Practices, Politics*. London: Verso.

Mosala, Itumeleng J. 1992. "The Implications of the Text of Esther for African Women's Struggle for Liberation." *Semeia* 59:129–37.

Philip, T. V., ed. 1982. *Krishna Mohan Banerjea: Christian Apologist*. Confessing the Faith in India 15. Madras: Christian Literature Society.

Prakash, Gyan. 1990. "Writing Post-Orientalist Histories of the Third World: Perspectives from Indian Historiography." *Comparative Studies in Society and History* 32, 1:383–408

Roe, James. 1965. *A History of the British and Foreign Bible Society*. London: British and Foreign Bible Society.

Said, Edward W. 1993. *Culture and Imperialism*. London: Chatto and Windus.

Sathiasatchy, P. A. 1991. "Interactions between the Faiths of Tamils as Reflected in Tamil Literature with Special Reference to Christianity." *Arasaradi: Journal of Theological Reflection* 4, 2:64–84.

Shohat, Ella. 1992. "Notes on the 'Post-colonial.'" *Social Text* 31, 32:99–113.

Soares-Prabhu, George. 1994a. "Anti-greed and Anti-pride: Mark 10:17–27 and 10:35–45 in the Light of Tribal Values." *Jeevadhara: A Journal of Christian Interpretation* 24, 140:130–50.

————. 1994b. "Two Mission Commands: An Interpretation of Matthew 28:16–20 in the Light of a Buddhist Text." *Biblical Interpretation: A Journal of Contemporary Approaches* 2, 3:264–82.

Stegemann, W. 1984. *The Gospel and the Poor.* Philadelphia: Fortress Press.

Thangaraj, Thomas M. 1990. "Towards a Singable Theology." In *Venturing into Life: The Story of the Tamilnadu Theological Seminary.* Ed. Samuel Amirtham and C. R. W. David. Madurai: Tamilnadu Theological Seminary, pp. 109–18.

Thoburn, Stanley C. 1961. *Old Testament Introduction.* The Christian Students' Library 24. Madras: Christian Literature Society.

Trinh, Minh-ha. 1991. *When the Moon Waxes Red: Representation, Gender, and Cultural Politics.* New York: Routledge.

Trivedi, Harish, and Meenakshi Mukherjee, eds. 1996. *Interrogating Postcolonialism: Theory, Practice, and Context.* Shimla: Indian Institute of Advanced Study.

Wickremesinghe, Lakshman. 1985. *Christianity Moving Eastwards and Other Papers.* Birmingham, England: Selly Oak Colleges.

Williams, Patrick, and Laura Chrisman, eds. 1993. *Colonial Discourse and Post-colonial Theory: A Reader.* New York: Harvester Wheatsheaf.

Winslow, J. C. 1923. *Narayan Vaman Tilak: The Christian Poet of Maharashtra.* London: SCM.

Witherington, Ben, III. 1987. *Women in the Ministry of Jesus.* Cambridge: Cambridge University Press.

Vandana, Sister. 1989. *Waters of Fire.* Bangalore: Asian Trading Corporation.

Young, G. M., ed. 1935. *Speeches by Lord Macaulay with His Minute on Indian Education.* London: Oxford University Press.

2

The Indian Textual Mutiny of 1820

The Brahmin, the Baptist, and Their Contested Interpretations of the Bible

This slim volume is worth whole libraries of so called great books of India. Keep it, young fellow, and study it.
　　　　　　— VIKRAM CHANDRA in *Red Earth and Pouring Rain*

[I]f you want to defeat the Englishman's power...burn his books.　　— VIKRAM CHANDRA in *Red Earth and Pouring Rain*

When the colonizers were engaged in civilizing the natives as part of the Enlightenment project, the popular perception was that the natives not only were hapless consumers of imperialized interpretations, but even collaborated with colonizers. I wish to contest this stereotypical notion, and in doing so will concentrate on a text produced during the Empire days, and on the interpretative clash it invoked. The text in question — *The Precepts of Jesus: The Guide to Peace and Happiness, Extracted from the Books of the New Testament, Ascribed to the Four Evangelists* (1820) — was produced by a Bengali Brahmin, Raja Rammohun Roy.[1] In resurrecting this colonial encounter, I wish to draw attention to the fact that it was one of the colonized, and a Hindu at that, who shaped the debate and set the parameters for this interpretative feud, and also to how his missionary adversary was compelled

---

1. He was also probably the first Indian to produce an original theological essay in English: "A Defence of Hindu Theism" in 1817. M. K. Naik regards this as the first original publication of significance in the history of Indian English literature (*A History of Indian English Literature* [1982; Delhi: Sahitya Akademi, 1992], 14). However, the credit for publishing first in English, though on a slighter theme, should go to Dean Mahomed. See Michael H. Fisher, *The First Indian Author in English: Dean Mahomed (1759–1851)* (New Delhi: Oxford University Press, 1996).

to try to measure up to the standards set by Rammohun Roy. Furthermore, we will use this textualized controversy as a template to mark out how the Bible was conceptualized and utilized in the debate. In conclusion, I will locate Rammohun Roy's textual insurrection within the discursive practices of postcolonial scholarship.

Raja Rammohun Roy (1772?–1833) was by any standards an extraordinary person and is generally regarded as the foremost reformer of modern India. His life and work were a striking illustration of the sociocultural complexity generated by the colonial occupation. He was actively engaged in both religious and social reform during the colonial period. He founded The Brahmo Samaj (Society of God), a Hindu ethical and religious reform movement. In the current climate of refashioning Hindu self-identity, the role played by Rammohun assumes legendary and mythical proportions. The standard biographies on his achievements naturally contain a fair share of imaginative speculations drawing on his English works and promoted by his English admirers. The autobiographical sketch which Rammohun himself produced further fueled the speculation (Rammohun Roy 1982:223–25; henceforth "EW"). A scholarly biography which comprehensively addresses the religious, philosophical, and cultural influences that undergirded his literary, theological, and social activities has yet to emerge.[2] For our purpose, let me sketch a few important biographical details relevant to the context of this chapter.

Rammohun Roy, a Rarhi Brahmin, was born in Radhanagar, Hubli, West Bengal. By birth, background, and education, he ranked many social stations above his theological opponents, the Serampore Baptist missionaries, who came from the British lower class and as nonconformists had nondescript status in colonial India. He came from a family which had acquired its wealth during the Moghul days. Besides his wealth, he was an erudite Indian with a good knowledge of Sanskrit and of Persian, the court language of the day. His mother, Tarini Devi, was credited with instructing him in Sanskrit. Later he received his Vedanta education from the Calcutta pundits Mrtyunjay

---

2. The present essay deals selectively with one aspect of Rammohun Roy's career which ensued after publication of the *Precepts*. For other facets of his colorful and often controversial life see Dermot Killingly, *Rammohun Roy: In Hindu and Christian Tradition, The Teape Lectures, 1990* (Newcastle upon Tyne: Grevatt & Grevatt, 1993); Bruce Carlisle Robertson, *Raja Rammohun Roy: The Father of Modern India* (Delhi: Oxford University Press, 1995); V. C. Joshi, ed., *Rammohun Roy and the Process of Modernization in India* (Delhi: Vikas Publishing House, 1975); Jatindra Kumar Majumdar, *Raja Rammohun Roy and Progressive Movements in India: A Selection from Records (1775–1845)* (Calcutta: Art Press, 1941), esp. xvii–cvi; Susobhan Sarkar, *On the Bengal Renaissance* (Calcutta: Papyrus 1985 [1979]), esp. 69–96; and Nalin C. Ganguli, *Raja Rammohun Roy* (Calcutta: YMCA Publishing House, 1934).

Vidyalankar and Sivaprasad Sarma. His father, Rankanta Roy, provided him with the kind of education sufficient to get employment in the Nawab's court, and did not at that time envisage English becoming the official language. After the establishment of a Supreme Court in Calcutta, however, English education was considered essential, and at the age of twenty-two Rammohun began to learn English, which proved to be of supreme significance not only for him as a colonial subject but for India's future as a colonized nation. Later, when he was embroiled with the Christian missionaries, he also mastered Greek and Hebrew, the latter learned in six months from a Jew.

Rammohun Roy was an insatiable student of comparative religion and was most challenging and provocative when it came to religious matters. He was probably one of the earliest Indians to interact theologically with Christian missionaries in the modern period, and was equally engaged in polemical debates with his own Brahmin pundits. His stay from the age of twelve to fifteen in Patna, a seat of Islamic learning, influenced his belief in one God and his rejection of idol worship. His later sojourn in Banaras, the citadel of Hindu learning and orthodoxy, led him to further criticize the Hinduism of his day, marked as he saw it by idolatry and superstition, and devoid of spiritual purity. When he was only sixteen he produced a manuscript, which has not been traced, in which he disapproves of Hindu idolatry. In his autobiographical letter, he notes that this tract, "together with my known sentiments on that subject, having produced a coolness between me and my immediate kindred," forced him to proceed on his travels (EW 224). This conflict, along with his "feeling of great aversion to the establishment of British power in India," resulted in his leaving his paternal home and India, and journeying to Tibet, where he became acquainted with Buddhism. His wanderings came to an end when he was welcomed back by his father and took up a post as a clerk in the East India Company at a time when British colonialism was beginning to make its intrusion — politically, militarily, culturally, and economically.

> I ... began to associate with Europeans, and soon after made myself tolerably acquainted with their laws and form of government. Finding them generally more intelligent, more steady and moderate in their conduct, I gave up my prejudice against them, and became inclined in their favor, feeling persuaded that their rule, though a foreign yoke, would lead more speedily and surely to the amelioration of the native inhabitants; and I enjoyed the confidence of several of them even in their public capacity. (EW 224)

The reasons behind Rammohun Roy's change of heart about the civilizing role of the British in India are not entirely clear. A simplistic and a cynical view attributes the change to Rammohun Roy's place among the urban elite, who benefited most from the mercantile and educational opportunities that accompanied colonial rule.[3]

When he arrived in metropolitan Calcutta in 1814, he was an unknown outsider, but his views on Hinduism, and the societal reforms in which he was engaged, such as sati, soon brought him close to a number of English administrators and Christian missionaries. His early contacts with the missionaries were cordial,[4] and the following remarks of Joshua Marshman (1768–1837),[5] the Baptist missionary at Serampore who later became his adversary, aptly describe not only what the missionary thought of him, but also Rammohun Roy's scholarly reputation, cosmopolitan background, and hermeneutical stance:

> Rama-Mohuna-Raya, a very rich Rarhee Brahmun of Calcutta, is a respectable Sanskrit scholar, and so well versed in Persian, that he is called Mouluvee-Rama-Mohuna-Raya: he also writes English with correctness, and reads with ease English Mathematical and metaphysical works. He has published, in Bengalee, one or two philosophical works from the Sanskrit which he hopes may be useful in leading his countrymen to renounce idolatry. Europeans breakfast at his house, at a separate table, in the English fashion; he has paid us a visit at Serampore, and at a late interview, after relating an anecdote of Krishna, relative to a petty theft of this God, he added, "The sweeper of my house would not do such an act, and can I worship a god sunk lower than the man who washes my floors?" He is at present a simple theist, admires Jesus Christ, but knows not his *need* of atonement. He has not renounced his caste, and this enables him to visit the richest families of Hindoos. He is said to be very moral; but is pronounced to be a most wicked man by the strict Hindoos. (Collet 1962:113; italics in original)

His endless controversies with his own Hindu pundits, or, as Rammohun Roy himself put it, "verbal arguments against the absurdities of the idolatry practised by them," his involvement in the abolition of sati, and his own endorsement of and recommendation of Jesus' teaching to his own people, would have made him a natural ally to the

---

3. For instance, see Sumanta Banerjee, *The Parlour and the Streets: Elite and Popular Culture in Nineteenth-Century Calcutta* (Calcutta: Seagull Books, 1989).
4. See Banerjee, *The Parlour and the Streets.*
5. Joshua Marshman was one of the famous trio of Baptist missionaries who worked in Bengal. The other two were William Carey (1761–1834) and William Ward (1769–1823). Serampore, a suburb ten kilometers north of Calcutta, was the epicenter of their missionizing activity.

missionaries' intention of rescuing the decadent Indians. In an early letter to John Digby, his one-time superior officer in the East India Company, Rammohun Roy wrote: "The consequence of my long and uninterrupted researches into religious truth has been that I have found the doctrine of Christ more conducive to moral principles, and more adapted for the use of rational beings, than any other which have come to my knowledge" (Collet 1962:109).

The Brahmin's Bible

However, it soon became clear that the missionaries and Rammohun Roy occupied different hermeneutical firmaments. The missionaries were incensed when his *Precepts* came out,[6] and most tried to dissociate themselves from it. According to his son, Marshman "considered it important to stand forth in defense of the vital doctrines of the Gospel" (Marshman 1859:238). From the vantage point of the twentieth-century writing on the life of Jesus, the *Precepts* was an innocuous text, if there ever is such a thing. It is a compilation of Jesus' moral sayings, largely based on the Synoptic materials, minus genealogies, miracle stories, historical incidents, and doctrinal narratives. It was a kind of Q document based on the King James Version. Like Tatian in his *Diatessaron,* Rammohun integrated the various Gospel narratives into a single narrative. Historians of biblical interpretation often credit D. F. Strauss with the first modern investigation of the Gospels, but that honor should go to Rammohun Roy, whose work predated that of Strauss by fifteen years. The *Precepts* starts with Matthew's Sermon on the Mount, and follows a redactive order of the Gospel. Then come Markan and Lukan materials, and finally an eclectic selection of John, including passages from chapters 3, 4, 8, 9, and 15.

The work also has an introduction setting out Roy's hermeneutical position. His objective was to present the essence of the gospel, which lies not in the doctrines, as the missionaries insisted, but in the moral teachings of Jesus.[7] In other words, he wanted to "free the

---

6. *The Precepts* was first published by Calcutta Baptist Press, run by a group of Baptists who were rivals of the Serampore Baptists. They also published Rammohun's first two defenses — *An Appeal to the Christian Public in Defence of the Precepts of Jesus* and *Second Appeal to the Christian Public in Defence of the Precepts of Jesus.* When the debate reached a boiling point, the Calcutta Baptists felt that Rammohun had gone too far, and they refused to publish his *Final Appeal,* which he published in a press set up by himself. See E. Daniel Potts, *British Baptist Missionaries in India, 1793–1837: The History of Serampore and Its Mission* (Cambridge: Cambridge University Press, 1967), 235 n. 4.

7. Interestingly, around this time and out of a different hermeneutical need, a similar

originally pure, simple and practical religion of Christ from the heathenish doctrines and absurd notions" (EW 921). He also wanted to purge the Gospel narratives of their miracles, which he called "heathen notions," because he believed that anyone who was rational enough to reject Hindu mythologies would find them unhelpful. In his view, the Christianity that the missionaries were propagating at the time was simply substituting one set of "polytheistical sentiments" for another. The implication was that he could improve the text and do a better job than the missionaries in presenting Jesus because they were obsessed with and trapped within their evangelical theology. When the controversy was raging between him and Marshman, Roy went on to accuse Marshman of actually degrading the dignity of the author of the text, Jesus (EW 694).

The introduction that Rammohun wrote to the *Precepts* sums up his position:

> I feel persuaded that by separating from the other matters contained in the New Testament, the moral precepts found in that book, these will be more likely to produce the desirable effect of improving the hearts and minds of men of different persuasions and degrees of understanding. For, historical and some other passages are liable to the doubts and disputes of free-thinkers and anti-christians, especially miraculous relations, which are much less wonderful than the fabricated tales handed down to the natives of Asia, and consequently would be apt, at best, to carry little weight with them. On the contrary, moral doctrines, tending evidently to the maintenance of the peace and harmony of mankind at large, are beyond the reach of metaphysical perversion, and intelligible alike to the learned and to the unlearned. (EW 484–85)

The *Precepts,* expunged of miracles, dogmas, and history, in Rammohun's view not only contained "the essence of all that is necessary to instruct mankind in their civil duties, but also the best and the only means of obtaining the forgiveness of our sins, the favor of God,

---

compilation of Gospel narratives was produced by Thomas Jefferson, the third President of the United States. It was called *The Philosophy of Jesus of Nazareth,* and has an intriguing subtitle: "extracted from the account of his life and doctrine as given by Matthew, Mark, Luke and John. Being an abridgement of the New Testament for the use of the Indians unembarrassed with matters of fact or faith beyond the level of their comprehension." The Indians referred to here are not the Native Americans, but Jefferson's code for his political opponents, the Federalists and their clerical allies, "whose political and religious obscurantism, as the president saw it, endangered the stability of the republic and needed to be reformed by a return to the simple, uncorrupted morality of Jesus." See Dickinson W. Adams, ed., *Jefferson's Extracts from the Gospels: The Philosophy of Jesus and the Life and Morals of Jesus* (Princeton, N.J.: Princeton University Press, 1983), 28.

and strength to overcome our passions, and keep his commandments" (EW 552).

Rammohun Roy was the one-man "Jesus Seminar" of his day. His quest was not so much for the historical Jesus, but for a Jesus acceptable and intelligible to the Indian mind. In scrutinizing the Gospel narratives, he was looking for the core teaching of Jesus. He exhibited supreme confidence in disconnecting essentials from nonessentials. Just as he had tampered with his own *Vedas,* so he did with Christian texts. Rammohun Roy did not see his selection of material as denigrating the Christian Scripture, or delegitimizing the sections he left out, but saw his hermeneutical venture as similar to that of Jesus himself, and even of the missionaries themselves. He pointed out that Jesus extracted, from among many, two commandments — love to God and love to fellow beings — and substituted them for all the law and the prophets. This in his view was "a sufficient guide to secure peace and happiness to mankind at large — a position that is entirely founded on and supported by the express authorities of Jesus of Nazareth" (EW 550). Moreover, he drew attention to the fact that the missionaries also were engaged in such selective textual reproductions, and with similar motives: to improve people morally and spiritually.

> [F]or we see very often extracts from the Bible, published by the learned men of every sect of Christians, with a view to the maintenance of particular doctrines. Christian churches have selected passages from the Bible, which they conceive particularly excellent, and well adapted for the constant perusal and study of the people of their respective churches; and besides, it is the continual practice of every Christian teacher to choose from the whole scriptures such texts as he deems most important, for the purposes of illustrating them, and impressing them on the minds of his hearers. (EW 559)

The Heathen and His Hermeneutics

What in effect the *Precepts* did was to invalidate the powerful pillars of evangelical Christianity — belief in the atonement, the doctrine of the Trinity, the divinity of Jesus, and the self-sufficiency of the Scriptures. Rammohun Roy wrested Jesus from his role at the focal point of missionary preaching, and reframed him as a wise and moral guide, as a "Messenger of God" and a "Spiritual Teacher" (EW 212), and as an agent of God who demonstrated to his followers not how to die but how to live. His aim was to liberate Jesus from the denominational, credal, and theological prisons into which he had been locked

by the missionaries. Just as he had tried to do with Hindu religious figures, he wanted to construct the figure of Jesus anew, because neither
the "image of Holy Jesus in Roman Catholic Churches, nor the representations of the Divine Ram in the Hindoo Temples, are identified
with either of those sacred persons" (EW 895). He situated Jesus as
one among many prophetic figures revealing the Almighty, and as one
who, with the prophetic figures before him, did not stake claims "to
be considered incarnations of the divine essence" (EW 589). His Jesus
was a literary construct based on textual traditions of the gospel.

It was not Rammohun Roy's intention to denigrate Jesus. Like many
Indians of the time, he had an affection and admiration for Jesus,[8] but
he saw his task as rescuing Jesus from the imperial portrayals, which
he regarded as travesties. He thought deifying Christ was both an af-
front to God and an anti-Christian doctrine (EW 873). Needless to say,
a construal of Jesus as a moral teacher did not go down well with the
missionaries at Serampore. The Serampore Baptists were products of
an evangelical and pietist revival who could not envisage Jesus exclusively as a moral guru without the doctrinal and miraculous motifs
seen as integral to the biblical witness. In Rammohun Roy they faced
an unexpected, unfamiliar enemy. In England, as dissenters, they faced
the strong theological arm of high-church Anglicanism, whereas in India they came up against an opponent who, from a different cultural,
religious, and linguistic position, threatened their cherished doctrines
and, far worse, made of the Bible, the supreme arbiter, a culturally
relative text. They were totally unprepared for such a theological
confrontation.

The textualized controversy between Rammohun Roy and Marshman had all the hallmarks of a colonial encounter wherein invader and
invadee were locked together in a new common history, growing up in
it and engaged with it, although unequally — with, for a change, the

---

8. Rammohun Roy's construal of Jesus was one among many mapped out by Hindus in
British India during the nineteenth century, in response to the missionaries' essentialist and
biased view of Hindus. See, for instance, the work of Keshub Chunder Sen, P. C. Moozumdar,
and Swami Vivekananda. These portrayals show affection and admiration for Jesus. Compared
to the then prevalent images of Jesus worked out by H. S. Reimarus (1694–1768), D. F.
Strauss (1808–74), and Ernest Renan (1832–92), marked by skepticism and an anti-Christian
slant which conceived Jesus as a sad, mistaken reformer, the portrayals by the Indians were
enthusiastic and positive, and projected a person worthy to be followed and emulated. For
a Christian appraisal of their work see M. M. Thomas, *The Acknowledged Christ of the
Indian Renaissance* (London: SCM Press, 1969), 1–98, 111–49. For a postcolonial reading of
their constructions see R. S. Sugirtharajah, "The Magi from Bengal and Their Jesus: Indian
Construals of Christ during Colonial Times," in *Images of Christ: Ancient and Modern,*
ed. Stanley E. Porter, Michael A. Hays, and David Toombs, Roehampton Institute London
Papers 2 (Sheffield: Sheffield Academic Press, 1997), 144–58.

colonized setting the ground rules. What effect Rammohun Roy's text would have had on the originally intended recipients, his fellow Hindus, is difficult to imagine. Rammohun Roy's claim that a Bengali and a Sanskrit version would follow did not materialize.

Marshman and Roy's hermeneutical engagement must be viewed against the social and cultural landscape of nineteenth-century England and India, when India was engaging with Western values and Christian ideals. It was undertaken against the backdrop of the colonial teleology of progress, when the institutions and customs of Indian society faced the competing claims of tradition and modernity. The attitudes of Marshman and Rammohun Roy to the Bible reflect the two worldviews they were representing — the premodern and modern respectively. This period saw the emergence of the Enlightenment and marked the advent of the modern period and its concomitant values — reverence for reason and belief in universal truths, human autonomy, scientific progress, and so forth. Premodern assumptions were called into question in every field — philosophy, history, science, and theology. Tools designed to interrogate these fields began to be applied to the Bible as well. This meant that the authority of the Bible, and so much more, came under scrutiny. This shift in understanding has been described by Hans Frei in *The Eclipse of Biblical Narrative* as the loss of the narrative sense of Scripture.

Rammohun Roy's production of the *Precepts* was a symptom and legitimization of the new mood — Scripture was one more object to be investigated. The interpretative key was reason. He wrote: "I appeal to the scripture, and also to common sense" (EW 825). For him, the texts themselves and not merely their interpretations had to be subjected to rational analysis. He believed in the authority of the Scriptures because they inscribed the unity of God. As later impositions by the Church, doctrinal configurations contradicted both Scripture and reason. Earlier he had arraigned mullahs and pundits for imposing doctrinal content on their original texts and for tampering with them to "promote their own interests" and "support their views," "under the name of traditions" (Majumdar 1941:189). Now it was time to indict the missionaries. Whereas the European thinkers of that time, Lessing, Semler, Reimarus, and others, contested belief in the supernatural and uncovered distortions and forgeries in the Scriptures, Rammohun Roy saw his task as purifying the texts from the subsequent intermixture of idolatrous and "polytheistical" ideas. Like Bultmann after him, Rammohun was trying to demythologize and demystify the texts of unpalatable elements.

Textual interrogation of this sort was not new to Rammohun Roy. He had been engaged in such a task earlier with the Vedic texts, which had naturally caused resentment among his own Brahmin pundits. For him both texts — Christian and Sanskritic — were corrupted by "subsequent intermixture of polytheistical ideas" (EW 680), *"both of them being equally* and *solely* protected by the *shield of mystery"* (EW 172; italics in the original). Although the authority of the Scripture was assumed, its veracity had to be validated by rational means. For Rammohun Roy, the Bible was an artifact, a product of faith, and as such had undergone "human distortions" (EW 823). Employing his own version of historical-literary method, he was able to demonstrate how doctrines propagated by the missionaries were products of evangelical Christianity, and totally opposed to the gospel represented by Jesus. He was able to show through his method that the texts addressed specific issues in specific contexts, and that they were not intended for all time. The only message that transcended this specificity was the twofold law of love to God and love to fellow humans.

At a time when missionaries were trying to utilize the Bible as a strategic resource to demarcate familiar colonial binaries, Christian and heathen, saved and damned, Rammohun Roy neutralized such dichotomizing perceptions by positing the *Vedas* and the Christian Scripture as part of a larger textuality, manifesting one revelation in two separate textual traditions. To quote him: "If the manifestation of God in the flesh is possible, such possibility cannot reasonably be confined to Judea or Ayodhya, for God has undoubtedly the power of manifesting himself in either country and of assuming any colour or name he pleases" (EW 908). Whereas missionary strategy had been to preserve the purity of the Christian Bible and dismiss other sacred texts as fatally contaminated, Rammohun saw both as containing pure and impure elements. As he was conversant with both Scriptures, he knew what he was talking about.

> I call on reflecting men to compare the two religions together and point out in what respect the one excels the other in purity? Should the *Christian* attempt to ridicule some part of the ritual of the Veds I shall of course feel myself justified in referring to ceremonies of a similar character in the Christian Scripture; and if he dwells on the corrupt notions introduced into Hindooism in more modern times, I shall also remind him of the corruption introduced by various sects into Christianity. But *a Christian* must know very well that such corruptions cannot detract from the excellence of Genuine Religions themselves. (EW 907, italics in the original)

He went on to demonstrate that the moral perfection and monotheistic claims made on behalf of the Judeo-Christian God are equally inscribed in the Vedanta. He argued that "the Vedanta, in common with the Jewish and Christian Scriptures... constantly ascribes to God the perfection of those moral attributes which are considered among the human species excellent and sublime" (EW 563). Later he went on to place the Vedanta above the Judeo-Christian Scriptures. He found the anthropomorphic descriptions of God in the Christian Scriptures theologically infantile, and the blood sacrifice to expiate the sins of humanity, demanded by the gospel, gruesome. Thus he felt able to elevate the Vedanta over other texts because it taught that the "only means of attaining victory over sin is sincere repentance and solemn meditation."[9]

Viewed in the light of today's scholarship, Rammohun Roy's method was far ahead of that of Marshman. Employing his own version of the narrative criticism currently in vogue among biblical scholars, he was trying to exercise the role of the reader and address the question of the effect of the narrative on its audiences. His attempt was an illustration of how a narrative can be transformed to suit the needs of an audience. He was trying to construct a text which would have a particular effect on the audience, namely, its Hindu readers. Marshman's interpretation, by contrast, was premodern, and cloistered in theological and denominational preconceptions.

Marshman's hermeneutical presupposition was determined by his evangelical theology. He envisaged the Bible as having one "grand design" and embodying the evangelical foundations such as the divinity of Christ, atonement, and the Trinity. His legitimate anguish was, "if the foundations be destroyed what shall the righteous do?" (Marshman 1822:65). His conception of the Bible was controlled by the basic tenets of evangelical Christianity. He would press into service the entire Bible from Genesis to Revelation to attest and legitimize the cherished doctrines of evangelical theology. Thus, he would see in the angel of Bochim (Judges 2) the figure of Jesus, and discern early signs of trinitarian elements in the writings of Isaiah.

For Marshman, the Scriptures were a "harmonious whole" (Marshman 1822:2), which cannot be broken. Marshman's attitude reflects a traditional Protestant, unquestioning view of the Bible. He found it difficult to accept any revelation besides that of the Bible or any possi-

---

9. Cited in David Kopf, "Rammohun Roy and the Bengal Renaissance: An Historical Essay," in Joshi, *Rammohun Roy and the Process of Modernization in India,* 27.

bility of salvation other than the one mediated through Jesus Christ. For him the text is prior, transcendental, and holds eternal values. It is an article of faith and as such the proper response is humble acceptance and veneration. In his view "a real Christian" should believe in "the Divine authority of the whole of the Holy Scripture" (Marshman 1822:6) and receive it as the "Word of God." In one of his replies to Rammohun Roy, Marshman wrote, "To us the Scriptures are sufficient" (253). His conception of the Bible as an infallible document comes through clearly when he keeps referring to it as "Sacred Oracles," "Sacred Writings," "Sacred Scripture," "Divine Writings," and "Divine Records" (147). The implication is that the words of Scripture are actual words spoken by God and therefore needing no interpretation.

For Marshman, the Bible is a unitary, coherent textual whole. Any attempt, such as that undertaken by Rammohun, to dissect the Scriptures was to strip them of their "peculiar majesty and authority" and to degrade them to "a level with the writing of men ... and they are no longer the power of God unto salvation" (Marshman 1822:8). In Marshman's view the Christian Scripture consistently conveys the same message: "It is not the voice of one writer merely, it is the uniform language of the Divine Writers through a period of nearly sixteen hundred years" (193). For him the wholeness of the Bible is reinforced by its doctrinal content. When Marshman talks about the unity of the Bible, he does not imply consistency and coherence among the various parts of the Bible. Rather, wholeness for him is something to be negotiated within the writing, determined by prior theological convictions. For him the basic evangelical tenets such as the doctrine of atonement and the divinity of Christ could be traced to five different sources — the Old Testament, the declarations of Christ, the evangelists, the apostles, and the book of Revelation, equal in authority but differing in clarity and fullness (Marshman 1822:82). For him the crux of the gospel is summed up thus: " ... that God views all sin as so abominable, that the death of Jesus Christ alone can expiate its guilt; and the human heart is so corrupt, that it must be renewed by the Divine Spirit before a man can enter heaven. ... But we may ask without these two dogmas what is the Gospel?" (10). In the later stage of the controversy, Marshman wrote:

> This body of evidence adduced, is not founded on one or two passages which criticism might hope to shake; it is founded on nearly Two Hundred different Testimonies, which nourished the faith and piety of the

true worshippers of God age after age. All hope of shaking it therefore is totally vain. Could one or two of these testimonies be invalidated — or ten or even twenty, this doctrine would still remain immovable. (193–94)

In short, Marshman was engaged in appropriations of the texts that were pietistic, sectarian, and hegemonic.

Invader and Invadee and Their Exegetical Enactments

For Rammohun Roy, exegesis is largely a literary, historical, linguistic, and rational enterprise. It involves a rigorous analysis of the context of ancient texts. In other words, scriptural passages have to be seen in their context, otherwise "they are liable to be misunderstood" (EW 637), and "if unconnected with their context, and interpreted without regard to the idiom of the languages in which they were written, may, as experience has shown, be adduced to support any doctrine whatever" (EW 692). For instance, worshipers of fire might justify their position by quoting Jesus' saying that he will baptize with the Holy Ghost and with fire (EW 617). For Rammohun the text functioned at two levels — literal and figurative:

> The mode of interpreting the Scripture which is universally adopted is this, that when two terms, seemingly contradictory, are applied to one person, then that which is most consistent with reason and with the context, should be taken in a literal, and the other in a figurative sense. Thus, God is declared to be immaterial, yet to have hands, eyes & c. The latter expressions taken literally, being inconsistent with reason, and with other passages of the Scripture, are understood as metaphysically implying his power and knowledge, while the former is interpreted in its strict literal sense: in like manner the term "Lord God" & c applied to another than the Supreme Being must be figuratively understood. (EW 631–32)

What Rammohun Roy was advocating was that the arbiter for right reading was not necessarily the internal scriptural evidence but that this had to be matched by reason and had to be seen in the light of what he called "the idiom of the language of Scripture" (EW 664). Such an approach allowed Rammohun Roy freedom in handling texts.

On the other hand, Marshman's efforts were not exegesis in the genuine sense, but a long stringing together of scriptural quotations. His exegetical response to Rammohun Roy was as if he were dealing with the Deists back in Britain: do not argue, but destroy their claims by quoting batches of scriptural texts. He mixes texts from different books of both testaments to make his point, thus denuding them of their complexity and variety. Marshman's interpretation was cloistered in his theological and denominational convictions. It was not exegesis at all but an assertion of power; or, as Rammohun Roy himself puts it, missionary interpretation was "preached by another body of priests, better dressed, better provided for and eminently elevated by virtue of conquest" (EW 201). In his view, "truth and true religion do not always belong to wealth and power, high names or lofty palaces" (EW 147). He clearly perceived a close interplay between interpretation and power. On another occasion he said that "there is a battle going on between reason, scripture and common sense; wealth, power and prejudice" (EW 918). Michel Foucault's observation on the close nexus between authority and knowledge has had a significant impact on current cultural studies. However, Rammohun Roy had identified the phenomenon and emphasized it long ago.

A striking aspect of Rammohun Roy's hermeneutical aim was his strong emphasis on putting the word into practice. "[T]here is no other means of attaining eternal life except the performance of our duties towards God in obeying his commandments" (EW 553). In his view, "forms and ceremonies were useless tokens of respect for God, compared with the essential proof of obedience and love towards him evinced by the practice of beneficence towards their [i.e., human beings'] fellow-creatures" (EW 551). His hermeneutical concern was with the ethical and practical meaning of Scriptures. He went on to remind Marshman that he could gather at least a hundred scriptural passages to validate his argument, but cited Matthew 25:31–46 as sufficient to prove his point (EW 553). What was remarkable was that he went on to reconfigure the doctrine of atonement, one of the cherished doctrines of evangelical theology, in terms of practical help and moral duty, rather than through the juridical images of expiation espoused by Marshman. This recasting, to quote Rammohun Roy, was justified since the Scriptures "teach us the performance of our duty to God and to our fellow-creatures and as the most acceptable atonement on our part to the All-merciful, when we have fallen short of that duty" (EW 572).

This intense practical orientation helps to explain why Rammohun Roy often shied away from doctrines, whether Hindu, Muslim, or Christian, based on speculation. For him the usefulness of the textual tradition of a religion is measured by the effect it has on the community. The interesting aspect of his hermeneutical engagement was that he began by promoting Christianity for its ethical, exemplary, and social values, but ended up cleansing its doctrines — the very template which the missionaries tried to use for missionizing purposes. For Marshman, the interpretative aim was how to formulate a doctrinal orthodoxy which would help to achieve the redemption of the heathen. His interpretative interest was what Scripture said about salvation and the means to achieve it. For the most part, Marshman brought to the text a soteriological question — what must the heathen do to be saved? He pointed out to Rammohun Roy that the leading doctrines of the New Testament "may be summed up in the two following propositions, that God views all sin as so abominable that the death of Jesus Christ alone can expiate its guilt; and that the human heart is so corrupt that it must be renewed by the Divine Spirit before man can enter heaven"; he went on to say that teaching Christianity to the natives of India "*without* them would have effected nothing; it must have left the Hindoos nearly as they were" (Marshman 1822:11; italics original). Unlike Rammohun Roy, the aim of interpretation for Marshman is not moral purity or practical engagement, but the assurance of personal salvation.

What is striking about the debate is that both exhibit an inherent biblicism. The text remains at the center of the debate over the legitimacy of their interpretation. Rammohun Roy's repeated claim was that he "sought to attain the truths of Christianity from the words of the author of the religion and from the undisputed instructions of his Holy Apostles, and not from a parent or tutor; I cannot help refusing my assent to any doctrine which I do not find scriptural" (EW 630). He believed in the authority of the Scripture and wished to restore the original text, for he believed that this was the only way to "guard against endless corruptions, absurdities, and human caprices" (Majumdar 1941:189). For Marshman, doctrines and practice are of "no value while we have Scripture themselves" (Marshman 1822:251). The one reads the Bible contextually, the other uncritically and pietistically. Both believed in the power of the religious texts of the past, and both saw them as repositories of significant meanings and drew upon them for human elevation. One substituted the Scriptures for the priest and urged readers to go to the text directly, unhindered by priestly interpretations, which keep the truth concealed "under the imposing veil of high-sounding expressions" (EW 680), whereas the other expected the believers to put their trust in divine revelation, denominational authority, and the interpretative control of the missionaries.

Both of them reduced the New Testament to neat doctrines predetermined by their hermeneutical stance. One conceived it as a manual for human living and the other saw it as a depository of doctrines. They were arguing on two different levels — the level of faith and the level of history. Whereas Marshman passionately admired the Jesus of faith, Rammohun Roy was morally heartened by the Jesus of history. He differentiated between the teachings of Christ and Christianity, the message of Jesus and the institutional and denominational garb in which it was presented. In another controversy, with R. Tytler, a lay person, Rammohun writes, "I appeal to History, and call upon the *Christian* to mention any religion on the face of the earth that has been the cause of so much war and bloodshed, cruelty and oppression, for many hundred years as this whose '*sweet* influence' he celebrates" (EW 907; italics in the original).

Marshman's interpretative strategy was in accord with many missionaries' representation of Indians as victims of Hindu religion and objects of missionary benevolence. From Rammohun's point of view, Indians were not victims; decadent they might be, but still possessed of an intellectual and spiritual capacity to renew themselves. In his controversial dialogue with Tytler, Rammohun Roy wrote:

> [W]ith respect to *Science, Literature, or Religion,* I do not acknowledge that we are placed under any obligation. For by a reference to history it may be proved that the World was indebted to *our ancestors* for the first dawn of knowledge, which sprang up in the East, and thanks to the Goddess of Wisdom, we have still a philosophical and copious language of our own, which distinguishes us from other nations who cannot express scientific or abstract ideas without borrowing the language of foreigners. (EW 906; italics in the original)

Rammohun Roy rescued the Bible from the scripturalists, and Christian faith from missionary doctrinal infighting. His target was not the Bible, but a narrow and selective form of interpretation. Rammohun Roy's presentation of the Gospels dismantled and destabilized the Christian texts in the form in which the missionaries were trying to promote them in India. It challenged the Bible's inherent assumptions.

In concluding this section, it is worth noting that Rammohun Roy's contribution lay not necessarily in destabilizing biblical texts or resisting imperial interpretations, but in reaffirming a forgotten and overlooked aspect of Christianity — namely, its component of praxis. Missionaries were reminded that in their overemphasis on the doctrinal aspect, they had largely forgotten the moral and ethical aspects of the gospel. This seemed to be the commonly held position of missionaries of the time. Rev. Deocar Schmid, of the Church Missionary Society, who in fact fired the first salvo in the controversy with Rammohun, considered "the religion of the Bible to be a mere system of doctrines unencumbered with morality."[10]

Rammohun Roy rendered a valuable service by reasserting an aspect of Christianity which missionaries were overlooking.

Colonial Clashes

Now to take up the question of the colonized calling the shots. Rammohun not only contested the imperial storytelling, but also all through the debate went on to reshape it. He had already engaged in numerous textual controversies with his own Hindu pundits when he took upon himself the task of editing the Hindu Scriptures, and was well prepared for this missionary encounter. Marshman, on the other hand, though he claimed that he had been studying the Bible for over thirty-five years (Marshman 1822:69), was a novice at theological disputes, let alone at literary productions concerning theological matters. His son recalls that in one of the letters that Marshman wrote during the controversy, he confessed: "[T]hese are the only articles in divinity I have ever written" (Marshman 1859:239). His inexperience came through clearly in his engaging in the debate as if India were a Christian country. Rammohun repeatedly reminded him of the folly of "introducing all the dogmas and mysteries taught in Christian churches to people by no means prepared to receive them" and referred to the missionaries as "so incautious and inconsiderate in their attempts to enlighten the natives of India, as to address the instructions to them in the same way as if they were reasoning with persons brought up in a Christian country, with those dogmatical notions imbibed from their infancy." (EW 557). One instance of Marshman's Eurocentric way of handling the contro-

---

10. See Rev. W. Adam's letter to Rev. William Yates, one of the Calcutta Baptist missionaries, on the original grounds of the missionary controversy with Rammohun Roy (May 1824), in Majumdar, *Rammohun Roy and Progressive Movements in India*, 65. The same Schmid who accused Rammohun Roy of interfering with the text had himself produced a summary of the Bible. To quote Adams again:

> In the compilation of this work Mr. Schmid has laid himself open to a charge of as serious a nature as that which he has with so little reason brought against Rammohun Roy. Although he professes to have composed it in the words of Scripture, yet he has not hesitated to make various additions which school-boys, converts, catechumens, and other natives for whom chiefly it is intended, will be apt to regard as of equal authority with the Scripture themselves.... Now although in the English part of the publication all these additions are distinguished from the language of Scripture by being printed in the italic character, yet in the Bengalee no such distinction is or can be used, and therefore all native readers, at least, are left to conclude that Mr. Schmid's additions are the words of inspiration. (Ibid., 61)

versy occurred when dealing with Rammohun's hermeneutical claims.
He counterattacked as if he were trying to handle Deists at home,
not engaging them in debate, but bamboozling them, as evangelical
Christians in England did, with a barrage of scriptural quotations.

At the beginning of their textual skirmish, it became clearly evident
who was going to call the tune. The deployment of the term "heathen"
was crucial to the debate. As a way of legitimizing European intervention, colonizers were actively involved in producing images which
reinscribed the cultural and religious differences between imperialists
and imperialized natives. One such image was of the "Other" as the
heathen — the antithesis of all civilized and Christian values. One interesting aspect of the debate was the deployment of the term by both
the colonizer and the colonized. At the beginning of the debate, Marshman called Rammohun Roy a "heathen." By using the term, part of the
imperial vocabulary of the time, Marshman was denying the possibility
that a native such as Roy was capable of intelligent articulation of religious matters. His was the rhetorical strategy of debasing the "Other"
and declaring the arguments of the native unworthy. It was an insensitive and injudicious move on the part of Marshman, for he was well
aware that Roy was a formidable scholar and a religious reformer at the
forefront of emancipating his own Hindu tradition from its superstitious
tendencies. Rammohun Roy found the use of the term "unchristian."
He appealed to the public to judge on the evidence of the text whether
the compiler of the *Precepts* was a believer or a heathen. Marshman further complicated the issue when he tried to defend his use of the term.
Though he disclaimed any uncharitable connotations in his use of the
word "heathen," he stuck to his narrow interpretation of a heathen as
one who does not accept "the Divinity and Atonement of Jesus Christ,
and the Divine authority of the whole of the Holy Scriptures" (Marshman 1822:6). In other words, a heathen is one who is outside the world
of civilization manifested by biblical vision and evangelical Christian values. Rammohun Roy was no passive recipient of this colonial
stereotype. He went further and claimed that it was the missionaries'
presentation of Jesus which was marred by heathen notions:

> I am sorry to say...the idea of a triune-God, a man-God, and also
> the idea of the appearance of God in the bodily shape of a dove, or
> that of the blood of God shed for the payment of a debt, seem entirely
> Heathenish and absurd.[11]

---

11. Rammohun Roy's letter to Dr. Ware, dated February 2, 1824. See *A Review of the Labours, Opinions, and Character of Rajah Rammohun Roy: In a Discourse on the Occasion*

He reappropriated the very term used by the missionaries, reframed it, and turned it against them. In his case, it was an ironic reversal. This changed not only the tone but the very nature of their interpretative feud. From then on Marshman refrained from using the term "heathen," referring instead to the writer of the *Precepts* simply as compiler, author, or by his name.

At the height of the debate, Rammohun tired of Marshman's routine repetition of Jesus as Jehovah God (EW 820), and urged him to follow the normal practices and methods established by Christians in studying the Bible. What is striking is that the interpretative techniques of the Judeo-Christian tradition, which were controlled by European missionaries, were now not only being taken over and creatively used by dissenting invadees, but redirected to the invader, and that these techniques were seen as the proper arbiter in the debate. In other words, the invader's weapons were appropriated by the invadee to confront the invader. Rammohun told Marshman that the only way to overcome the sectarian bias which had colored Marshman's interpretation was to first study "the Old Testament as found arranged in order, and to acquire a knowledge of the true force of scriptural phrases and expressions," and "then to study the New Testament, comparing the one with the other" (EW 666).

Marshman accepted the instructions and seriously and faithfully followed them, and then informed Rammohun Roy: "We have now met our author on his ground, in complying with his own suggestions examined the books of the Old Testament in their order respecting the *Deity* as well as the Atonement of the Son of God" (Marshman 1822:193; italics in the original). He realized that he had been handicapped; he went on to admit that "this has deprived us of those advantages which arise from selecting and condensing evidence" (193). The irony is that the debate shows the colonizer competing with the colonized and trying to measure up to him and emulate him. Marshman, who used to deploy a veritable barrage of biblical passages, admits defeat. The interesting aspect is that the invadee not only acquired the invader's weapons of criticism, used them to interrogate the invader's story, exposed the invader's tricks, challenged the invader in his totality, and revealed his nakedness, but also provided him with hermeneutical clothes to cover his nakedness. Instead of ending as an abusive exchange in the master's language, that Rammohun Roy

of his Death; a Series of Illustrative Extracts from his Writings; and a Biographical Memoir, ed. Lant Carpenter (London: Rowland Hunter, 1833), 57.

turned the weapons back at the invader offered the emperor a set of hermeneutical clothes which never quite fit him.

Another instance of turning the tables was Rammohun Roy's reinstatement of Jesus as an Asiatic. Colonial racial stereotypes played a key role in the imperial interpretations. Imperial discourse projected the image of the manly Englishman and the effeminate Indian/ Bengali (Sinha 1995). Missionaries, who often helped to shape the colonial social forms of the time, often also ridiculed Indians as persons "degraded by Asiatic effeminacy" (EW 906). By searching for the historical Jesus of the Gospels, Rammohun Roy was trying to portray him as an Asiatic. In so doing, he was reminding the missionaries that "almost all the ancient prophets and patriarchs venerated by Christians, nay even Jesus Christ himself, a Divine Incarnation and the *founder* of Christian Faith, were ASIATICS, so that if a Christian thinks it degrading to be born or to reside in *Asia* he directly reflects upon them" (EW 906; italics and capitalization in the original). By repositioning Jesus within his western Asian milieu, Rammohun Roy was reminding the missionaries that the Jesus they projected was not an Englishman, and that the Christian message they promoted was by no means an English people's religion, because Jesus himself was an Asiatic and reflected the sentiments and ethos of Asians.

Rammohun Roy outscored Marshman in another respect. Whereas Rammohun Roy was impelled to think comparatively and contrastively, Marshman resorted to a sectarian, partisan, and rigid Christian form of polemics. The conspicuous difference between Rammohun Roy and Marshman lay in the former's dexterity in situating side by side Hindu, Muslim, and Christian texts as an interconnected textual continuum, whereas the latter operated principally on a monoreligious and monotextual basis and did not feel the need to incorporate the Bible into a wider textuality. Rammohun Roy claimed to discern the manifestation of the Divine in an extended web of textuality. His mastery of different traditions enabled him to shift between sacred texts and bestride a diverse religious heritage. This gave him a decisive edge over Marshman. When missionaries overplayed the degrading aspects of popular Hinduism, he was able to counterattack, drawing attention to equally unattractive features of Christian faith practiced at a popular level. Once he threatened:

> If a Christian were to insist on . . . corruptions as the standard of Hindooism, then a Hindoo would also be justified in taking as the standard of Christianity, the system of religion which almost universally pre-

vailed in Europe previous to the fifteenth century of the Christian Era, and which is still followed by the majority of Christians (namely, Catholics, Greeks, Armenians) with all its idols, crucifixes, Saints, miracles, pecuniary absolutions from sins, trinity, transubstantiation, relics, holy water, and other idolatrous machinery. (EW 194)

He could point out to Marshman that Hindu, Jewish, and Christian texts describe God both as incomprehensible and in figurative terms. He could cite texts from both religions to prove his case. He writes: "It is, however, very true, that the Vedanta declares very often its total ignorance of the real nature and attributes of God. Kenopanishand, ver. 3: 'Hence no vision can approach him, no language can describe him, no intellectual power can compass or determine him: we know nothing how the Supreme Being should be explained,' & c. It also represents God sometimes in a manner familiar to the understanding of the vulgar. Mundaka, ch. vii, sect. 1: 'Heaven is the head, and the sun and moon are his eyes; space is his ears' & c" (EW 563). Similarly, he could show that such contradictory claims are not peculiar to Hindu texts alone but are manifested commonly in the biblical tradition.

But such declarations are not peculiar to the Vedanta doctrines, as these are found frequently in the Sacred Scriptures. Job XXXVI:26: "Behold God is great, and we know him not." Ch. XXXVII:23: "Touching the Almighty we cannot find him out: his greatness is unsearchable."...In the Old Testament, as well as in the New, God is represented as... having arms with hands and figures; a head, with face, mouth, tongue, eyes, nose, ears; a heart, bowels, back, thighs, legs; as seeing, being seen, speaking, and hearing, slumbering, waking, & c. (EW 563–64)

The comparative approach enabled Rammohun Roy to argue that both textual traditions contained elevating as well as degrading elements. He was able to demonstrate how such an approach, coupled with the combination of modernism and traditional values, allowed an indigenous faith like Hinduism to assert and adapt itself in the face of an onslaught from outside. Marshman, on the other hand, saw the sacred writings of the Hindus as exclusively polytheistic, irrational, chaotic, and anomalous, made up of "cunningly devised fables" (Majumdar 1941:52). In Marshman's view, "the Vedant among the Hindoos have totally failed in suppressing idolatry, when, amidst all their sublimity, they so completely foster human pride and sins of the heart" (Majumdar 1941:52). For these reasons, he called Rammohun Roy "injurer of the cause of truth" (EW 549). Marshman's investment in a particular theological stance and his complacent approach to the Bible as a universal civilizing force left him ill-equipped and caused him to fail in his arguments. Rammohun Roy, on the other hand, was not confined to a monocentric approach and was able to move the interpretative discourse toward a more complex interplay of competing texts.

As the debate progressed, Marshman lost his nerve and his tone become shrill and vitriolic. This was evidenced in one of the last replies he wrote in *Friend of India.* In the December 1832 issue of the quarterly he condemned Rammohun Roy to eternal death "unless he take refuge in the death of Christ" (reproduced in Majumdar 1941:55). Rammohun Roy, on the other hand, was generous and wished for the well-being of the missionaries.

> I hope no one will infer that I feel ill-disposed towards the missionary establishments in this country. This is far from being the case. I pray for their augmentation, and that their members may remain in the happy enjoyment of life in a climate so generally inimical to European constitutions; for in proportion to the increase of their number, sobriety, moderation, temperance, and good behaviour have been diffused among their neighbours as the necessary consequence of their company, conversation and good example. (EW 560)

The *India Gazette* had followed the debate between the Brahmin and the Baptist, and included an editorial in its May 17, 1824, edition which gives a clue as to the eventual winner:

> [T]he attack on Rammohun Roy . . . really appears to us to have been about as injudicious and weak an effort of officious zeal as we ever heard of. The effect of that attack was to rouse up a most gigantic combatant in the Theological field — a combatant who, we are constrained to say, has not yet met with his match here. (Reproduced in Majumdar 1941:72)

These words written by a Christian eloquently sum up the stature and personality of Rammohun Roy.

Colonial to Contemporary

Looking back at the interpretative skirmish between Rammohun and Marshman, there is nothing particularly original in their approaches to the Bible. Biblical scholarship has moved on since their hermeneutical duel, and neither of them would be able to recognize the innovative ways in which the discipline has redrawn its map.

Our interest in their use of interpretative strategies lies less in their hermeneutical creativeness than in the particular cultural milieu in which they were enacted. Their textual controversy assumes a different configuration and significance when it is seen against the nineteenth-century colonial complexities of occupation and enslavement. One of the significant contributions of postcolonial scholarship has been to devise theoretical frames for studying the implications of colonialism from the perspective of the colonized. Such scholarship looks in particular at how the invadees have worked out different sets of negotiations to articulate their identity and nationhood under subjugation. How did they dissolve the differences between the self and the invading other? Mimicry? Assimilation? Hybridization? Mary Louise Pratt has come up with helpful terms — "contact zone" and "transculturation" — to describe such an interface. In her book *Imperial Eyes* she explains this contact zone as "space of colonial encounters, the space in which peoples geographically and historically separated come into contact with each other and establish ongoing relations, usually involving conditions of coercion, radical inequality, and intractable conflict" (Pratt 1992:6). By deploying the term "contact," her intention is to substitute the one-sided charting of colonial history of the imperialists with ideas of interlaced co-presence and intertwined discourses. The other term, "transculturation," is a phenomenon and characterization of the contact zone. Transculturation, according to Pratt, is "how subordinated or marginal groups select and invent from materials transmitted to them by a dominant or metropolitan culture" (6).

From a postcolonial perspective, the discursive clash between Rammohun Roy and Marshman emanates from a site which Pratt would term a contact zone — "the spatial and temporal copresence of subjects previously separated by geographic and historical disjunctures, whose trajectories now intersect" (Pratt 1992:7). Here two people distinctly separated by religion, language, culture, and caste lodged together unequally, but with the invadee eventually gaining the upper hand. The way Rammohun Roy co-opted the normative text of the imperialist, and delegitimized it and projected it back to him, would be characterized as a "transculturation" in the "contact zone."

In the cultural milieu of the nineteenth-century missionary-imperial enterprise, the Bible was constituted as a colonial book, aligned with specific theological and missiological practices. Through the strategy of selection and redaction, Rammohun Roy transformed and reconstituted the text and placed it in an altogether different and wider intertextual hermeneutical field. He countered the univocal authority of the colonial book by transposing it onto a multitextual and multi-religious tradition. His innovative and often eclectic selection and reconceptualization goes through what Pratt calls a process of trans-culturation — a process whereby marginal or subordinate groups select and create new cultural forms from materials transmitted to them by a dominant or an invading culture. What the *Precepts* did was to challenge an invasive, imported text and its assumptions from the "margins," thus exposing its universalizing tendencies. Rammohun's book transformed the totem text of Christians through various strategies of selection and adaptation, thereby undermining its canonical status and its association with the invader's culture. What the *Precepts* demonstrated was that, although Rammohun did not have control over what material could go into the canonizing process, at least he could determine what material could be selected for a new situation and the purpose for which it might be used.

What was striking about the controversy, in conclusion, was not the resistance that Roy provided, nor that he was brave enough to answer back, but the vital questions he raised in the course of the textualized debate. The legacy of the clash is the hermeneutical direction he set for Indian Christian theology. It is interesting to note that it was set by a Hindu. The questions he raised are still with us — the search for an Asian Jesus undefiled by European manners and customs, the re-covery of the praxiological aspect of the gospel, the intertextual nature of sacred texts, the interplay between discourse and duty, and the significance of India's religions for articulating Christian theology. These questions are still with us and dominate our thinking. Or, as the narrator in Shashi Tharoor's novel *The Great Indian Novel* would have put it: "Oh, Ganapathi, there was no escaping from these questions! I tried to tell myself that answers were irrelevant, that the questions had to be asked differently" (Tharoor 1990:374).

Works Cited

Chandra, Vikram. 1995. *Red Earth and Pouring Rain*. London: Faber and Faber.

Collet, Sophia Dobson. [1900] 1962. *The Life and Letters of Raja Rammohun Roy*. Ed. Dilip Kumar Biswas and Prabhat Chandra Ganguli. Calcutta: Sadharan Brahmo Samaj.

Majumdar, Jatindra Kumar. 1941. *Raja Rammohun Roy and Progressive Movements in India: A Selection from Records (1775–1845)*. Calcutta: Art Press.

Marshman, John Clark. 1859. *The Life and Times of Carey, Marshman, and Ward: Embracing the History of the Serampore Mission.* Vol. 2. London: Longman, Brown, Green, Longmans & Roberts.

Marshman, Joshua. 1822. *A Defence of the Deity and Atonement of Jesus Christ in Reply to Ram-Muhun Roy of Calcutta.* London: Kingsbury, Parbury, and Allen.

Pratt, Mary Louise. 1992. *Imperial Eyes: Travel Writing and Transculturation.* London: Routledge.

Rammohun Roy, Raja. [1906] 1982. *The English Works of Raja Rammohun Roy.* Ed. Jogendra Chunder Ghose. 4 vols. New Delhi: Cosmo Publications. [Cited as "EW."]

Sinha, Mrinalini. 1995. *Colonial Masculinity: The "Manly Englishman" and the "Effeminate Bengali" in the Late Nineteenth Century.* Manchester: Manchester University Press.

Tharoor, Shashi. 1990. *The Great Indian Novel.* New Delhi: Penguin Books.

3

Imperial Critical Commentaries

Christian Discourse and
Commentarial Writings in Colonial India

*Books are the Missionaries of the future, for the printed page
knows no frontiers, can speak all languages, enter closed lands,
pass through closed doors, and is often the only means of
communicating the truth.*

— SHASHI THAROOR in *The Great Indian Novel*

*Basic truth about the colonies... Any time there is trouble, you
can put it down to books. Too many of the wrong ideas getting into the wrong sorts of people. If ever the empire comes to
ruin, ... mark my words, the British publisher will be to blame.*

— SHASHI THAROOR in *The Great Indian Novel*

The series of biblical commentaries known as the "Indian Church
Commentaries" was produced in India in the early years of this century, at the "high noon" of empire. These commentaries were a project
of the Anglican Church in the subcontinent, and were published in ac-
cordance with a resolution of the Synod of Indian Bishops in 1890.
All of them on New Testament books, they were written by, to use
Edward Said's phrase, "Orientalist residents" — Anglican bishops and
missionaries who had the lived experience of and actual contact with
India and her people, her religious and cultural traditions.[1] The series

---

1. There were nine titles in the series: T. Walker, *The Epistle to the Philippians*, 1906
(hereafter *Philippians*); T. Walker, *The Acts of the Apostles*, 1919 (*Acts*); Arthur Crosthwaite, *The Second Epistle to the Corinthians*, 1916 (*2 Corinthians*); H. U. Weitbrecht Stanton,
The Gospel according to St. Matthew, 1919 (*Matthew*); H. Pakenham-Walsh, *The Epistles of
St. John*, 1921 (*John*); W. K. Firminger, *The Epistles of St. Paul the Apostle to the Colossians
and to Philemon*, 1921 (*Colossians and Philemon*); E. F. Brown, *The First Epistle of Paul
the Apostle to the Corinthians*, 1923 (*1 Corinthians*); E. H. M. Waller, *The Revelation of*

was first produced under the supervision of A. M. Knight, the Bishop of Rangoon, and G. A. Lefroy, the Bishop of Lahore. Later, it had C. F. Andrews as the general editor, who was noted for his friendship with Mahatma Gandhi and for his open advocacy of Indian independence, a rare and a remarkable trait among the missionaries of that time. When Andrews resigned in 1913, L. E. Brown of Bishop's College took over as general editor. The general preface, written by the Bishop of Lahore, Lefroy, spells out the intention of the series:

> It is hoped that these commentaries, while presenting a direct and scholarly interpretation of the New Testament, based upon the work of the great English Commentators, will, at the same time, contain such references to Eastern religious thought and life as may make them serviceable to both Christian and non-Christian.[2]

The expectation was that these commentaries, written in English, would eventually be translated into Indian vernacular languages.

In approaching these commentarial texts produced by writers who had considerable residential experience in British India, I would like to attempt the following: to situate the commentaries over against the English critical scholarship out of which they emerged; to uncover the exegetical practices which legitimized colonial intervention and presence; to map the very aggressive streak of Christian faith they sought to develop; and to provide illustrations of how they essentialized and fixed India. In conclusion I will reflect on how these commentarial texts help to illuminate the manner in which the missionary commentators were enabled and at the same time constrained by the colonial power-relations and ideologies of the time.

Gentlemen Scholars and Their Hermeneutical Manners

The writers of the Indian commentaries faithfully followed the format and the hermeneutical parameters set by leading English biblical critics of the time, such as J. B. Lightfoot (1829–89),[3] B. F. West-

---

St. John the Divine, 1926 (*Revelation*); and W. H. G. Holmes, *The Epistle to the Hebrews,* 1929 (*Hebrews*). All were published by SPCK Depository, Madras. Second editions of some of these volumes were published in London by SPCK. Moody Press, Chicago, brought out Walker's *The Acts of the Apostles* in 1965, which had a new introduction by Wilbur M. Smith but excised all references to India.

2. In some prefaces, the word "Western" is substituted for "English."

3. Lightfoot himself encouraged missionary enterprise and with Westcott and Hort was on the committee at Cambridge that founded the Cambridge Mission to Delhi. When the British Christians were disheartened and disappointed at early failures and the paucity of converts, he drew parallels between the early Church's missionary activities and the mission endeavors

cott (1825–1901),[4] and F. J. A. Hort (1828–92). As any student of nineteenth-century biblical studies will be aware, these three men occupied a quite distinctive niche in that period, and Cambridge, where they worked, was known as the "home for commentaries" (Elliott-Binns 1952:62). At a time when newly emerging German critical practices were rattling the sedate landscape of British biblical scholarship, these gentlemen scholars advocated a reasonable and restrained application of the new tools. While the popular perception of these methods was of a rationalist attack on the cherished beliefs of Christians, these English scholars mobilized the very same methods to reinscribe the central authority of the text and to validate the traditional teachings of the Church, thus helping to soothe the fears of the faithful. Stephen Neill, who was himself an Anglican bishop in Tinnevelly (a diocese in South India where Walker, one of the contributors to the series, worked), in his study of the history of biblical interpretation, points out that the Cambridge trio — Lightfoot, Westcott, and Hort — consciously worked out exegetical methods which differentiated them from the accepted German practice of the time (Neill and Wright 1988). While the Germans were stressing the philological details of the Greek words and the importance of the Greek syntax as a way into the meaning of the text, their English critics were keen on developing a native British tradition which went beyond merely using languages and lexicons. While the Germans had a single allegiance, namely to their discipline, the English had multiple loyalties, not only to academic learning but also to their Church traditions, and more

---

of his time and reminded them how a feeble and insignificant group of early Christians later flourished and spread in spite of obstacles and difficulties. About India he had this to say: "India is our special charge, as a Christian nation; India is our hardest problem, as a missionary church" (1896:91). Lightfoot felt in dealing with India the missionaries had been "too conventional, too English." He continued, "We must become as Indians to the Indian, if we would win India to Christ." He never explained how this was to be done (1896:92). See "Comparative Progress of Ancient and Modern Missions" (1896:72–92).

4. Among the Cambridge triumvirate, Westcott had a special interest in India. He believed in the conversion of India as the gateway to the rest of Asia. He wrote: "The conversion of Asia is the last and greatest problem which has been reserved for the Church of Christ. It is through India that the East can be approached. It is to England that the evangelising of India has been entrusted by the providence of God." See his *On Some Points in the Religious Office of the Universities* (1873:42). In keeping with the spirit of the times, he believed in the Empire and saw it as God's providence and as a preparation for the unity of all humankind. He also believed that each nation had a specific role to play in this divine scheme, and he had no doubt as to the role that had been assigned to Britain: "God has set us to be not only conquerors, or pioneers, or masters, or furnishers of the materials of outward civilization, but, beyond all, evangelists" (*Christian Aspects of Life* [1897:144]). He anticipated that the most subtle and discerning commentary on St. John's Gospel would be written by an Indian. For Westcott's theological, personal, and ideological involvement with India and her religions, see Martin Maw, *Visions of India,* Studies in the Intercultural History of Christianity 57 (Frankfurt am Main: Verlag Peter Lang, 1990).

significantly, to the ordinary Christian believers and their Christian feelings. They were trying to weave together the demands and expectations of serious biblical scholarship, Christian faith, and the Christian public. Daniel Pals, who investigated the portraits of Jesus constructed during the Victorian period, observes: "Like his colleagues in other disciplines, the biblical scholar at Oxford or Cambridge worked within a network of overlapping loyalties. There were ties to his pupils, his college, his university; ties to the Church and the religious sensibility of the populace. Placed only alongside these, not above them, were the claims of one's discipline" (1982:148). English biblical scholars saw it as part of their task to popularize their findings. Following the example set by the English critics, these Indian commentaries were an attempt to close the gap between the scholar and the ordinary reader.

In their acceptance of current German scholarship, the English critics reiterated that any interpretation must be critical, linguistic, historical, and exegetical, but also, in resistance, they added their own conditions, that it must be theological and pastoral. Stephen Neill observes: "To these general principles, however, the Cambridge Three added one further principle of the greatest significance. Their work was to be done from 'faith to faith'" (1988:94). The writers of the Indian Church Commentaries, who were all actively involved in the Christian cause of propagating the faith, went further and advanced another purpose for interpretation, that it be missiological. They perceived the Bible as a missionary tract, a self-help manual for missionary activities. Thus, Weitbrecht Stanton calls the Synoptic Gospels the "first missionary manuals" (*Matthew* 629). He goes on to reiterate this missiological intention: "The missionary work of the Church is the necessary consequence of the authority conferred on Jesus by the Father. Belief in Jesus involves a belief in missions" (715). Walker found Philippians to be characterized by a strong missionary spirit. "*Evangelistic zeal* is writ large on every page of it" (*Philippians* 20; italics in original). Interestingly, all these commentaries had a section called "Lessons for India," where easy parallels between the early church and India are not only drawn, but missiological significance is reasserted. Walker writes: "We may expect, therefore, to find in it [the book of Acts] clear lines of guidance for the conduct of similar work in India, and to learn from it useful lessons bearing upon our own circumstances and needs" (*Acts* xlvii). He pursues this further: "The object of each chapter is to guide the study of the scripture passages, to point out the chief missionary principles involved in them, and to supply illustrations from the mission-field as to their modern application" (9). *The Church Missionary Review,* an influential missionary journal of the time, hailed Walker's *Acts of the Apostles* as "an illuminating illustration of how the principles of the Apostolic age may be applied to the needs of the mission-field."[5]

Cumulatively these commentaries mirror the distinctive style and mood of the British biblical scholarship of the day. Victorian biblical critics, under the influence of the educationalists of the time like Matthew Arnold, saw their task as building character, promoting gentlemanly behavior, inculcating genteel manners, and improving moral conduct. Raising men useful to church and state, and fit for the various duties of life, were seen as significant hermeneutical tasks. Owen Chadwick supports such a notion:

> Though the university cannot help begetting a few professors, its true function is the nurturing of citizens, of gentlemen, of Christians. By its mathematical discipline it trains them in logic, by its physics it opens to them the order and beauty of creation, by its studies in ancient history and literature it brings them into converse with minds of philosophic power and literary imagination, by its religious teaching and pastoral care it fosters the virtue without which no state can stand. (1970:440)

The influence of these ideals found its way into the Indian commentaries. They spoke relentlessly about the moral improvement of the Indian people. But they had an additional agenda — to build a cadre of Indian Christians who would set an example to their morally suspicious and confused Hindu neighbors. Here is a typical passage from Weitbrecht Stanton: "The ideal Christian life is not like the Hindu, supposed to consist of four Ashrams or stages (religious student, householder, hermit, religious mendicant); the Christian has to develop the outer and inner life, practical and contemplative, together" (*Matthew* 614). Walker further undergirds the point: "With so much untruthfulness of speech and unrighteousness of conduct on every side of us, we Christians of India need to be very 'straight.' By rectitude of conduct let us protest against bribery, corruption, false evidence, questionable litigation, and any and every deviation from strict truth and equity. Above all, let us see to it that our hands are clean" (*Philippians* 70). Later he says, "We should seek to drink so deeply of the 'mind' of Christ that our deportment, especially before non-Christians, may be attractive and gracious, and our looks and words, and actions may be marked by true courtesy" (122). In Holmes's view the

---

5. *The Church Missionary Review* 63 (October 1912): 631.

only way the Christian community, as a minority community in India, could preserve its purity was through "the faithful application of discipline" (*Hebrews* 263). The commentaries seek out and identify what they deem to be evils of Indian society — superstition, mendacity, laziness, and bribery; all of these have to be resisted. In setting such moral boundaries between Indian Christians and other Indians, the commentaries served to establish the case for the British intervention. By prescribing Christian morality, these commentaries became the textual means for justifying the British occupation as the harbinger of civilization. In other words, Christianity was presented as a necessary appendage to the process of modernization, promoting a progressive outlook and contributing to alternative models of social behavior.

The Indian Church Commentaries were modeled on the "Cambridge Bible for Colleges and Schools," and it was this Cambridge Schools series that provided the main exegetical thrust and framework. The Indian Church Commentaries, like their Cambridge models, utilized the exegetical practices of the time, namely to open up the texts through historical criticism, or higher criticism as it was then known. The methods that were commonly available at that time were form, source, and literary criticism. The commentaries were erudite, dense, and pedantic, and were so preoccupied with providing the minutest of details that they seemed to lose the sense of the whole. They display all the hallmarks of historical criticism as it was practiced then. The text was lionized and venerated. It was seen as the "ultimate court of appeal" (*Acts* 154). The Bible was perceived as the repository of God's deeds and a record of God's word, and through its pages humanity was called to faith and obedience. It was seen as containing the historical evidence for Christianity, and as such it had to be read with a strong emphasis on the historical context. The meaning of the text resided either in the intention of the author or in the historical world represented by it, or both, and through the judicious use of historical inquiry one could get a glimpse of the original author and the first readers/audience and recover the original meaning. In other words, these commentaries manifest modernist notions of reason, history, philology, and a commitment to interpret the biblical narratives against their contextual milieu, paying close respect to the intricacies of the biblical languages. Contrary to the belief that the application of historical-critical methods undermined the authority of the text, the affectionate way the commentators handled the texts served only to increase their manifest reverence for the Bible and its clear importance for them.

I would like to end this section by drawing attention to an English characteristic embedded in these commentaries. The commentators exhibit a certain boyishness, a characteristic which Sir Ernest Barker identified as distinctively English (1995:55–63).[6] This "eternal boyishness" leaves space for fun, and these commentaries are peppered with witty and entertaining comparisons. Generally, of course, the commentaries are sober and restrained in their style, but occasionally they sparkle with this British style of playful humor. To illustrate, in commenting on the Matthean parable of the house built on sand, Weitbrecht Stanton refers to the palace of the Nawab of Mamdot, which was built on the sandy edge of the River Sutlej, and which collapsed during the rainy season (*Matthew* 216). The tearing of the robes by the high priest at the trial of Jesus is likened to an English judge putting on the black cap before condemning a criminal to death (*Matthew* 668). Walker, in describing the topographical relation of Corinth to Athens, tells his readers: "It was only fifty miles distant from Athens; but to go there from that university city was like passing from Oxford to London; or, in a certain sense, moving from Benares to Calcutta" (*Acts* 387). The feeling between the Pharisees and the Sadducees is compared to that between the Shia and Sunni sects of Islam (*Acts* 489). Anyone who is keen, enthusiastic, or extreme is depicted as a Brahmin. For instance, the priests of Baal are Brahmins of India (*Hebrews* 38); the Pharisees are the orthodox Brahmins of Judaism (*Acts* 530), or like the Wahhabi sect among the Mohammedans, who were known for their zeal for the Qur'an and for their occasional clashes with the political authorities (*Matthew* 87). Damaris is seen as an Indian devadasi — a temple dancer (*Acts* 386). Timothy, offspring of a mixed marriage between an Asian and a European, is described as a Eurasian (*Acts* 340). A Roman procurator is seen as equivalent to an Indian collector (*Matthew* 674). Pilate going to Jerusalem during the festival is like an Indian collector visiting a chief place of pilgrimage during a religious *mela* (*Matthew* 674). Herod's calling of an assembly of scribes when troubled by the wise men's query about the newborn king is likened to a Mohammedan ruler consulting his muftis (*Matthew* 64). Such hermeneutical pranks are instances of this English playfulness, in the sense of allowing scope for play in treating serious subjects. Perhaps these pranks relate to the well-known English love of nonsense — though they do also function as a form of cross-cultural

---

6. Six English characteristics identified by Sir Ernest Barker are social cohesion, eccentricity, amateurism, a sense of voluntary service, gentlemanly behavior, and eternal boyishness.

explication, and in this respect are often effective and helpful. Ernest Barker's observation on amateurism as characteristically English may also have its relevance here, in the sense that these missionaries were not professional biblical scholars.

Reframing Christianity

Edward Said's observation on how the Orient as a cultural contestant helped to define Europe (or the West) as its contrasting image, idea, personality, and experience (1985:2–3) is strikingly true of Christianity's relation to other faiths as presented in these commentaries. The books serve to map out a religious landscape in which Christianity is placed at the center. The primacy of the Christian gospel was assumed and seemed natural. The male, white colonial theological interpretation of the assumptions and ideals of the gospel is fully highlighted by placing it next to Hindu, Buddhist, Islamic, Sikh, and tribal values. Christianity's integrity, practicality, and historical nature are contrasted with Hinduism and its devious and idolatrous practices, its tyrannical doctrine of karma or rebirth, its basis in legends, and its violent caste system. Thus, not surprisingly these commentaries persistently fall back on binary distinctions of Christians and heathens, believers and unbelievers, "us" and "them." The construction of the demonized "Other" serves to validate the superiority of the Christian faith. The unfamiliar sights and sounds associated with Hindu religious practices are perceived as antithetical to Christianity and are therefore presented as inferior to Christian religious practices. The effect of all this is to establish British dominance, and to provide the moral imperative for imperial intervention, subjugation, and the prolongation of the British presence in a heathen land.

Muscular Christianity

Fundamental to the Christian imperialist's discourse is the assessment of the Indic faiths as inadequate and perverse in relation to Christianity. The commentaries repeatedly tell the readers that the salvation offered by Christianity is not like the Hindu idea of liberation from misery or escape from reincarnation, but is "complete deliverance alike from the guilt (2 Cor. 5:18, 19; Eph. 1:7) and from the power of sin (Matt. 1:21; Luke 1:74, 75; and Rom. 6:14) in the present life" (*Acts* 127). Whereas Hinduism induces pessimism, "Christianity inspires hope" (*2 Corinthians* 98, and also see *Hebrews* 141). Holmes goes on to describe the Hindu experience of salvation as a deep "state of coma" whereas the Christian conception is one of "conscious blessedness of the love and service of God" (*Hebrews* 195). For Hindus miracles are "mere wonder," but for Christians they are a "manifestation" of "spiritual force" and an illustration of "spiritual or moral lesson" (*2 Corinthians* 244). The peace offered by Hinduism and Islam is fatalistic, passive resignation, whereas Christian peace is fellowship with God through the communion of the Holy Spirit (*Philippians* 119). Hindu Scriptures have little relation to daily life whereas the Christian Scriptures offer solutions to the daily difficulties and problems of the people (*1 Corinthians* xlvi).

Hindu doctrines and religious practices are painted as vain, speculative, impractical, and useless. Commenting on the Christian understanding of knowledge, Walker writes:

> We must distinguish this "spiritual knowledge" from the "Jnana" of Hinduism. The latter, which is regarded as the "summum bonum" or highest attainment of religion by thousands in India, denotes rather a cold, philosophical knowledge derived from abstract meditation. The former indicates a spiritual grasp of the truths of revealed religion by a warm responsive heart, such a grasp as elevates the whole man. (*Philippians* 38; see also p. 93)

Similarly, Crosthwaite makes a distinction between Hindu and Christian understanding of asceticism since these two faiths depend on different conceptions of the nature of God and of human personality (*2 Corinthians* 235), while Weitbrecht Stanton, faced with similar birth stories in other religious traditions, tries to elevate the biblical virgin birth over the others:

> Stories of the virgin birth of an avatar or guru are to be found in Buddhism, Hinduism and other religions, but they differ from the Gospel narrative (1) in their wild and fanciful details compared with its self-restraint and sobriety; (2) in the absence of the idea of purity and sinlessness which is the very life of the story; (3) in the absence of an accredited series of prophecies which find their fulfilment in this event; (4) in the fact that the historical existence and character of the women concerned has no such attestation as that of the Virgin Mary. (*Matthew* 52)

The commentators work on a theological hierarchy with Christianity at the top and other religions placed underneath it as imperfect and inferior and needing to be cleansed and purified.

The *Gita* is the concentrated essence of Hinduism. It is the expression of all the highest hopes, aspirations and ideals of the best Indians that ever lived.... The book is to be read as a spiritual autobiography of Hinduism. Now the chief feeling that finds expression in the *Gita* is the desire for an incarnate Savior, a Savior incarnate for the good of men, incarnate to give a clear revelation of the will of God. The definiteness of the idea and the passion with which it is urged stand out in extraordinary contrast with the baselessness of the Krishna story.... The thought that remains in the mind after the perusal of this great work, is this — The *Gita* is the cry of the Hindu people for an incarnate Savior. (*2 Corinthians* 86)

The inference is that the other religions are waiting to be completed and corrected by the coming of Christ.

Christianity is presented as a historical, practical, and relevant religion, whereas the other faiths are projected as ritualistic, idolatrous, and superstitious: "Judaism, as followed by the Pharisees, was pre-eminently a system of ritualism and externalism; and Hinduism, Buddhism and Muhammadanism are, for the most part, similarly characterized" (*Acts* 530). In Weitbrecht Stanton's view, the Qur'an was a legal code devised by Mohammed, which, though it "had its uses for Arabia in the seventh century is clearly unsuited for the Western world in the twentieth, but the gospel of Jesus is as applicable to the twentieth century as to the first" (*Matthew* 154). The Hindu texts are seen as depositories of rules and ritual codes: "[I]n the Brahmanas, or its monistic code as contained in the book of Manu and other Dharmsastras, we are confronted with a network of rules and observances which enter into every detail of the Hindu's religious and social life" (*Acts* lxxv). These commentaries keep making the point that Indic religions, including Islam, have outlived their purpose largely through contact with Christianity and Western education. "Hinduism and Muhammadanism are perishing," claimed Crosthwaite (*2 Corinthians* 48 and 37). The Christian task is seen as getting rid of these outmoded practices and thinking:

The work of the Church in India must include the pulling down of the strongholds of systems, such as caste and some forms of philosophy, which are either false or have outlived their day of usefulness. All such destructive work, however, as St. Paul insists... is preparatory to construction on sounder lines. (*2 Corinthians* 206)

One of the strategies the commentators employed is their use of the classic self-understanding of Christianity as a historical religion based on the Incarnation and the Church as its continual manifestation: "Yet the process of manifestation, potentially complete in Jesus Christ, still continues in the world. Christ lives in and through His body the Church.... In the Church we have an 'extension of the Incarnation'" (*2 Corinthians* 38). Dismissing the Indian understanding of Incarnation as *lila* or *maya* and devoid of any historical element, commentators present Christian revelation as the supreme ground of all moral and theological value in which higher truth is embedded. Translated into the imperial Indian context, this meant that it was the Church's task to channel the spiritual energies of the people Britain ruled toward the manifestation and the establishment of God's Kingdom on earth.

In an attempt to meet the charge that Christianity had been founded comparatively recently, the commentators were eager to present Christianity as an ancient religion, as "eternal" as Hinduism. In exegeting 1 John 1:2, Pakenham-Walsh defends Christianity's ancient past: "St. John would not, therefore, allow that Hinduism or any other religion is older than Christianity. All truth is eternal: and the message we Christians have is as eternal as God Himself" (*John* 5). The prevailing assumption was that although Indic faiths might be ancient, they were static and nonprogressive, and could not be compared to the dynamic and evolutionary development of the Christian gospel.

The commentaries, though unashamedly triumphalistic, also project Christians as victims. Waller's rereading of the book of Revelation undergirds this projection. Certainly, the Book of Revelation is not easy to read. It weaves together myth, politics, history, praxis, and a vision of the future. Its background is political, religious, and economic and depicts a clash between a tiny powerless Christian community and the vast Roman Empire. Instead of reading it as a literature of good news for the victims, sustaining them with the hope of God's intervention, Waller redraws the map of a collective victimhood to include not only the minority Indian Christian converts but also the missionaries and the worldwide Christian Church, who are being oppressed by the menacing presence of Hinduism and other worldly powers. The beast is read not as a historical figure but as a symbolic representation of all the worldly powers in any age who rely on force and superstition in persecuting the Church of God (*Revelation* 265). The solution to this persecution is the establishment of the Kingdom in the future. Christians have been chosen for a glorious deliverance from the coming cataclysmic onslaught.

The great multitude, all united together in praising God for their redemption (chap. v), the countless multitude which no man can number
out of every nation, united before the throne of God (vii), the Bride
of Christ triumphing while earthly kingdoms and unions of men are
destroyed — these are pictures of the ideal Church which may well inspire us to effort and work, in order to bring to pass something of what
St. John saw. (*Revelation* 24–25)

The encouragement to endure the present oppression in anticipation
of future prosperity in another place and in another time conveniently
provides for the conservation of unequal social relations between the
invader and the invadee.

The commentaries underplay the social concern of the gospel and
its predisposition toward the poor. Pakenham-Walsh discounts these
concerns as "trivial" in comparison to a death on behalf of sinners
(*John* 83). As befitted a missionary who ended his days as chaplain at
Hampton Court Place, Firminger spiritualizes the poor: "The merit of
poverty, however, lies not in the want of money, not even in the limi-
tation of earthly desires which penury enforces, but in the devotion of
the poor man to God who alone can satisfy, and does indeed satisfy,
the empty soul" (*Colossians and Philemon* 217). Weitbrecht Stanton
concedes the importance of caring for the poor, but in his view this
should not interfere with "prayer and the ministry of the word" (*Matthew* 386). For him the "only true and lasting" philanthropy is union
with Christ (*Matthew* 626). The commentators, in other words, ad-
vocate a pietistic and personal form of Christian faith rather than a
Christian concern for the uplift and betterment of the underprivileged.
Though the missionaries were engaged in social welfare, they seemed
to shift in focus when it came to establishing the right priorities. Instead of coalescing the social and spiritual elements of the gospel, the
commentaries tend to emphasize the latter.

Needless to say, the definition of the gospel that the commentaries
come up with merely recapitulates the hallmarks of the evangelical
tenets of the time — the divinity of Christ, belief in the Triune God,
and the atonement.

We must humbly but faithfully proclaim the distinctive doctrines and
the Gospel in India, without either compromise or accommodation.
There must be no "toning down" of the great truths of the Trinity in
unity, the Divinity of Christ, the vicarious sacrifice of Calvary, the Personality of the Holy Ghost, under an amiable, but mistaken, idea of
meeting the prejudices of Hindus or Muhammadans. (*Acts* 106–7)

The Christian faith that these commentaries perpetuate falls within what today's scholars of theology identify as the exclusivist stance — Christianity as the only pointer to God.

> Christianity is exclusive, in that it is the final and complete revelation of God; as inclusive, in that it includes and fulfils every fragment of those partial revelations by which God was preparing the world through ages "by divers portions and in divers manners" for the final revelation in the Son. (*Hebrews* 91)

Gentle and Gentrified Christ

Viewed against the robust and vibrant christological images propounded by a number of Bengalis at that time, the figure of Jesus these commentaries present is tame, mild, and conservative. While Bengalis like Rammohun Roy, Keshub Chunder Sen, and P. C. Moozumdar, all members of the Brahmo Samaj, a Hindu reform movement, tried to rescue Jesus from denominational, doctrinal, and colonial entanglements, and recast him as an Asiatic and an Oriental figure, these commentaries warn their readers of the folly of such attempts at indigenization.[7] In Weitbrecht Stanton's view, "to patch an old garment of Hinduism and Islam with fragments of the teachings of Christ is self-destructive" (*Matthew* 250). The commentaries formulate a Jesus unsullied by Hindu, Islamic, or nationalistic overtones. Citing the example of how Judaizers' insistence on Jewish customs in Philippi impeded the spread of the gospel, Walker warns against such repetitions in India: "Let us beware in India, least we rear up Christians bound about with Hindu grave-clothes, or Muhammadan grave-clothes, or Caste grave-clothes, or National custom grave-clothes" (*Philippians 43*).

To counteract the Brahmo Samajists' attempts to incorporate Jesus into an Indian religious framework, one of the missionaries' strategies was to project the Indic religions as proleptic and transitory, waiting for fulfillment in Jesus Christ. Echoing the fulfillment theory worked out by J. N. Farquhar (1861–1929)[8] at that time, the commentators reconstruct Jesus as the one who satisfies the longings, ideals, and aspirations of many cultures, lands, and peoples. All other revelations are defective, preparatory, and provisional: "All lesser lights, God's revelation in the law, and the prophets, in non-Christian literature and philosophy, in men's most noble aspirations, in nature — are fulfilled in the true light, Jesus Christ, who Himself is the source of all these

---

7. See chap. 2, n. 8, for relevant literature.
8. See especially his *The Crown of Hinduism* (London: Oxford University Press, 1912).

reflected lights" (*John* 34). Crosthwaite defines how "one of the most important tasks of the missionary is the tracing of the way in which God has, in non-Christian lands, been preparing men for the coming of Christ, so that they may see that in Him the veil which lay over their past has been done away" (*2 Corinthians* 60).

What we see in these commentaries is the gentrification of Jesus. The figure of Jesus the commentators devise is an English gentleman who is an example to all. He is stripped of his oriental characteristics and reconfigured as a mild-mannered English gent. His greatest virtue is obedience: "He obeyed, even to the death; so then it is your bounden duty to obey, following his footsteps" (*Philippians* 65). In contrast to Hindu gods such as Rama and Krishna, who are devalued as ahistorical and mythical, Jesus is portrayed as a flesh-and-blood middle-Englander who loves the rural landscape. Walker observes: "Our savior is a lover of nature" (*Matthew* 200). Jesus is reconfigured as a detached person, holding no views on important issues of the day, as apolitical and without opinions. He maintains silence when it comes to pertinent questions about war or politics: "As in the case of civil and criminal justice, so with the military profession, our Lord did not pronounce any opinion as to the legitimacy of their methods, more especially as to the rightness or wrongness of war" (*Matthew* 222; also 662). As a gentleman, he is benevolent up to a point. He does not identify with the economically poor, but with those who are sick. His main task is seen as that of a healer who cares for the needs of individuals and heals both their physical ailments and the sickness of their souls (*Matthew* 121); such acts provide the most convincing argument that he is the Savior.

He is also presented as an English snob who observes social gradations and favors honors and titles. The Empire was consolidated among other things by the handing out of titles and rewards. Walker points out that the use of titles and honors was common in British India (*Acts* 571). Jesus is perceived as a respecter of titles and rank. On exposing Matthew 23:8–10, "Be not ye called Rabbi," Weitbrecht Stanton informs his readers: "Our Lord certainly does not mean to forbid the use of conventional titles of respect, as the Society of Friends have supported" (*Matthew* 572). For Weitbrecht Stanton, Jesus goes on to say that there is nothing wrong with the system as such, but that the fault lies in the people who chase after titles: "Jesus then does not condemn the use of conventional titles of honor, but the lust for them..." (*Matthew* 573). Put another way, it is Jesus the gentleman who is projected as the human and divine ideal.

Leave to Enter: Christian Citizenship

In the commentaries, and in the imperial discourse in general, we find competing visions of Christian citizenship. On the one hand, Christianity is presented as forging a "brotherhood" and as a witness in a heathen land, but on the other hand, it is presented as a preparation for an otherworldly existence. In concert with the prevailing modernist notion of grand-narratives, the commentaries reinforce the ideal of universal "brotherhood" and go on to claim credit for an achievement under British rule, which the Roman Empire with all its power failed to achieve — to unify its subject people in India, through the efforts of the Christian Church. A universal brotherhood, knitting together diverse groups of people, was seen as a great achievement.

> The Christian body is to be one great and united brotherhood, witnessing for Christ in a land where division and disunion have been so rife, and where the strife of races and castes has been so strong and constant.... National prejudices, racial animosities, and caste distinctions are to yield before a higher force.... Let us, therefore, draw closer together heart to heart and shoulder to shoulder, and shew to India the greatest object lesson she has ever seen — the vital union, in one loving holy brotherhood, of Eastern and of Western, of Brahman and of Pariah, of Aryan and Dravidian, of all contributing something towards the rich comprehensiveness and multiform character of the universal Church. (*Acts* lxix–lxx)

Crosthwaite, too, sees this unification as a positive contribution of the Christian Church: "This is still the strength of the Christian Church. It unites those whom many things after the flesh separate, the high caste and out-caste, the Indian and the European" (*2 Corinthians* 103).

At the time when Walker's commentary on Acts was published, India had its first visit from King George V and his Queen Mary. In a sermon preached on the eve of the durbar, the Bishop of Madras, basing his text on Revelation 9:1, spoke not only of the role of the Church and the Empire in building up this brotherhood, but described the gathering at the durbar as a foretaste of things to come:

> There are high barriers and deep gulfs that separate race from race and class from class in our Empire, and the one Power that can enable us to bridge the gulfs and break down the barriers is the love of God and the power of the living Christ in our hearts and lives. God grant that this power may be ours. May this great gathering at Delhi of so many races and peoples united in one common sentiment of loyalty to our King-Emperor be the foreshadowing of a still higher Unity in the days

to come, when, through stress and storm, through conflict and self-sacrifice, through faith and love, we move steadily on towards the final goal when brotherhood becomes no longer an ideal but a reality.[9]

Indians who were perceived as unruly, vulgar, and diverse were being transformed into an orderly, well-mannered, and kindred Christian community with one faith, one Church, and one Lord. Speaking in the voice of liberal imperialism, these commentaries seek to include the Indian subjects within the imperial fold, while at the same time designating them as inferior. Through conversion, Indians could be incorporated into the brotherhood, as long as they acknowledged the rulers as their natural protectors. In incorporating the Indians into the universal "brotherhood," the commentators were not being egalitarian, but engaged in what Gramsci would call a hegemonic activity, that is, securing the consent of the governed through intellectual and moral manipulation rather than through military force (1976:57). In the case of the missionary commentators, one may add theological manipulation as well.

Scripting India

There are a number of ways in which a colonizing power consolidates its hold and position. It will emphasize the radical difference between the invader and the invadee. It will stress the savage nature of the natives to vindicate the right to occupy their country and subdue them. It will characterize them as subservient so that they can be subjugated and made to serve. It will label them as innocent so that they can be dominated by the invaders, and as untrustworthy so that no one will trust them. Throughout colonial history, such stereotypes of the native have been continually worked and reworked, confirmed and reconfirmed.

Arjun Appadurai has identified three distinct trajectories that tend to underlie the Western construction of the Orient — exoticism, essentialism, and totalism (1988:44). The commentaries provide instances of all three.

Exoticism

One way to legitimize cultural imperialism is to promote the notion of difference between the colonizer and the colonized. The commentaries routinely stress the differences between Indian and European

---

9. *The Church Missionary Review* (April 1912): 206.

religious landscapes. India is seen as a land where "the popular cultus consists chiefly in the worship of deities who are dead men apotheosized, and the religion of the most thoughtful lies in the pantheistic direction of speculations..." (*Philippians* 94). Indians venerate cows and worship bulls (*Acts* 168), and indulge in blood sacrifice (*Hebrews* 38). They also pay obeisance to the Sun and the Moon (*Acts* 169). Pakenham-Walsh's perception of India is as a land of degrading sights, "nautches, indecent sculptures and pictures, cock-fighting, etc" (*John* 47). It is a country where people's lives are controlled by astrology and horoscopes (*Acts* 169). For those coming from a monocultural background, India's religious, communal, and linguistic plurality seemed negatively exotic. India was seen as "a conglomeration of peoples [rather] than a homogeneous nation" (*Philippians* 57). Such disarray invites the introduction of Christianity and justifies the presence of the invaders. Indian religious, cultural, and linguistic plurality was not seen as something to be affirmed and celebrated but as competing and conflicting realities which needed a stabilizing core. This core, the commentaries claimed, could only be provided by British imperialism and its missions, which were seen as a benevolent intervention: "It is the glory of the Gospel that it is capable of welding together elements which are naturally heterogeneous and opposed" (*Acts* 137). Crosthwaite reiterates: "India's thought and life are like Indian music. There is much melody and many strains of great beauty, but no harmony. Our Lord comes as the Music Master to teach this" (*2 Corinthians* 156).

Essentialism

Essentialism is a way of imputing and characterizing the fundamental aspects of the "Other" so that it becomes susceptible to certain kinds of management. Certain practices — the caste system, idolatry, polytheism, religious rituals, temple dancers, mantravadis (magicians), and devil dancers — are invoked as Indian essences which are changeless and timeless. Walker points out to the readers that the "mantravadis and devil-dancers are legion" in India, and "exorcism is one of the main businesses" (*Acts* 413). He also warns his readers of the unmistakable presence of polytheism and idolatry "which now everywhere abound" (381), and views idolatry and fornication as entrenched in the Indian religious system (329). Religion is seen as endorsing the system of devadasis or temple dancers (329–30). In trying to essentialize India, the commentaries fixed India as backward, decadent, and in need of civilization, thereby justifying the British occupation as a civilizing and rescuing mission.

Totalism

Totalizing makes specific features of a group, namely its values, practices, and thought patterns, not only its essence but also typical of the community as a whole. The commentaries identify some features of Indian society and make them an embodiment of the entire country. Commenting on the reference to four thousand assassins at Acts 21:38, Walker writes: "We know, in the East, how frequently numbers are exaggerated through lack of mental accuracy" (*Acts* 472). Other totalizations contained in the commentaries include:

- Weeping and wailing is an Eastern custom where the emotion is released openly and uninhibitedly (*Acts* 452).

- In the East noon is the time for siesta (*Acts* 196).

- People in the East read aloud (*Acts* 197).

- Indians are meek and mild (*2 Corinthians* 216).

- Indians are unreliable and fail to keep promises. "In India the practice of putting the name down on a subscription list, and then never paying the amount promised, is very common" (*2 Corinthians* 179).

- In Indian courts witnesses can be bought over (*Matthew* 666).

- The Indian priests are corrupt and "known to fatten on religious endowments and contributions" (*2 Corinthians* 184).

- Indian church workers have a tendency to use church money for private purposes (*Philippians* 77).

- Indian society is debt-ridden (*Philippians* 129).

- Indian women are quarrelsome. Commenting on the two women, Euodia and Syntyche (Phil. 4:2), Walker portrays them as ringleaders and laments how many disputes in Indian congregations are instigated by women (*Philippians* 112).

Such portrayals are not surprising. They replicate the European Orientalists' notion of the time.

Framing Indians: Replication of the Colonial Stance

Indians are portrayed in these commentaries as innocent, emotional, and childlike, but at the same time devilish. The inference is that the natives require taming, civilizing, and converting through the active intervention of paternal imperialism. The Indian Church is often portrayed as an "infant church" (*Philippians* 20). In expositing the Johannine text which addresses the readers as little children,

Pakenham-Walsh comments: "The line of safety for India lies in accepting as 'little children' the light and truth which God has revealed" (*John* 177; also 44). The use of fictive parental-filial relationships was one way of integrating missionaries into Indian society. Missionaries were often addressed as Iyah (Father). Assuming the father's role, the missionary's influence extended to arranging marriages, finding employment, and settling Indian converts in the mission compound. The commentaries infantilize the Indians by treating them as children in need of edification instead of encouraging them to take control of their lives by rejecting dependency. At a time when serious political discussions were going on and self-rule for India was beginning to be debated, the commentarial image of the childlike Indians paternalistically affirmed that they were not ready for self-government.

The role of the Indians in these commentaries is very interesting. The converts are divided into two categories: the English-speaking and Western-educated, and the native Indians who speak in vernaculars. The former are seen as progressive and enlightened, the latter as provincial, nationalistic, conservative, and caste-oriented (*Acts* 137). Though these commentaries were written for the Indians, the Indians remain largely silent. The commentators speak for the Indians and represent them. We are told that educated Indians are ashamed of "vain ceremonies and idol-worship" (*Philippians* 20). When, on rare occasions, Indians speak, the commentaries incorporate statements which suit the theological agenda of the missionaries and are sympathetic to the imperial cause. Crosthwaite reports the statement of a nameless Indian convert: "India wants *love*. You can do anything you like with the people of this land if you only love them and show them that you do" (*Philippians* 110; italics original).

Pakenham-Walsh recounts an incident. When translating 1 John 3:2, the Indian pundit who was assisting the missionary found the language "too bold and the hope too magnificent." "No! it is too much," he said, "let us write that we shall be permitted to kiss his feet" (*John* 67). The commentaries cut out dissenting Indian voices, and the colonizer constantly seeks for confirmation of his colonial motive. The consolidation of colonial power is mediated through the presence of the colonized. Any native who exhibits a contrary knowledge not only threatens the colonial enterprise but also questions its very validity and presence.

These commentaries also show ambivalence toward the Indian theological and cultural heritage. Though these commentators believed in the primacy of Christian faith and the superiority of Western literature and European knowledge, they could not deny that Indian thinking had contributed to the enhancement of the theological and cultural knowledge of the world. The writings of leading Indians like Rabindranath Tagore, Kabir, Tukaram, and Ananda Coomarasawamy are cited with admiration. Sample passages from India's sacred and legal texts like the *Rig Veda,* the *Dhammapada,* the *Bhagavad Gita,* the *Bhagavata Purana,* and *Manu* are cited. The contributions of Sankara and Ramanuja, India's foremost philosophers, are also acknowledged:

> In no land has religious speculation been more rife than here in India. Hindu sages and philosophers have thought deeply and subtly, and attempted to unravel the intricate secrets of being, both human and divine. The result is a series of Sastras and "Darsanas" in which their deductions have been reduced to systems, each of which has its devoted followers. (*Philippians* 119)

Brown concedes that the Indian religious literature has been admired by the world, but this has not enabled Indians to grasp the mystery of God (*1 Corinthians* 35, 36). Though there is appreciation of some aspects of Indian culture and philosophy, to commentators the missionary intervention was justified on the grounds that such thinking had produced an array of conflicting systems: "But it is surprising to · find their conclusions are disappointing and mutually conflicting; so that, while some are theistic, others are atheistic; while some recognize the existence of human spirit as a fact, others see in it only a virtual image or reflection of the impersonal Divine Spirit" (*Philippians* 120). Such a state of cultural, religious, and theological anarchy provided the avenue for presenting the Christian gospel as a unified, homogeneous entity, thus privileging it over India's pluralistic, local, and often competing religious traditions.

At times, the commentaries invoke stereotypical images to pass judgment not on the "Other," but on the self. English character is seen as aggressive, energetic, and manly, viewed as at variance with the tone of the gospel. Indians, on the other hand, are perceived as less aggressive and less assertive, and in tune with the spirit of the gospel. To illustrate this difference Crosthwaite provides an anecdote from the time of the Indian mutiny. A holy man for a long time observed silence with a view to finding God. When bayoneted by a British soldier during the rebellion, he broke his silence with the words: "And thou too art He" (*2 Corinthians* 216). The holy man's passive resistance is celebrated and cherished as the supreme example of the "meekness of Christ." In other words, rather than summoning the negative images to restate the superiority of Christianity and Western malehood, commentators on this occasion call upon them to fuel a critique of British manners and customs:

> The natural temperament of the European makes for him meekness hard to acquire, and he often fails to attain it or see its strength. With the Indian this is not so, it may be that it will be part of the mission of the Indian Church to show the world afresh the beauty and the strength of the meekness and gentleness of Christ. (*2 Corinthians* 216)

The negative images of Indians are now not only recast as a virtuous universal model for Christian behavior, but also enlisted to recover and restore lost Western traits.

Revering and Rescuing Indian Women

These commentaries demonstrate their deepest contradictions in the construction of Indian womanhood. On the one hand, they show a genuine concern for the plight of Indian women, but on the other hand they prescribe only solutions entrenching marriage and domesticity. The plight of Indian widows is often highlighted as an instance of India's indifference to its own people's suffering. When commenting on the neglect of the widows by the early Church, Walker immediately sees a parallel in the Indian context: "One woman out of every six in this land is a widow, and nearly four hundred thousand girls under fifteen years of age belong to this class, their lot often being pitiable in the extreme" (*Acts* 138). Such conditions enabled the colonizing project to present itself as a form of improvement, liberating the people from poverty and ignorance.

The commentators have no qualms in enlisting the support of Hindu religious texts, which on other occasions they denigrate as sacred nothings, to support the traditional role of women. For them the ideal woman is Sita, the heroine of the Hindu epic *Ramayana,* seen as "India's model of wifely devotion" (*2 Corinthians* 155). Indian women are seen as victims of Hindu and Islamic oppression and objects of missionary compassion: "India, with its teeming female population, calls loudly for Christian women who will break the trammels of 'custom' and courageously carry the Gospel to their Hindu and Muhammedan sisters. When souls are perishing, we must do and dare something to help them, even if we seem to go against 'custom' in so acting" (*Philippians* 114). Crosthwaite warns that such liberation might undermine family values and increase the divorce rate: "Christianity's higher ideal of womanhood must in the long run raise the standard of social purity in India, but the liberation of Christian women creates special dangers and problems. It is the Church's duty to make a firm stand against the lax views on divorce which have made such headway of late" (*2 Corinthians* 139). The liberation of Indian women was aimed not at reordering inequitable gender relations or social hierarchy, but at inviting them benevolently into the nobler cause of the civilizing mission. Conversion was advocated as a means of crossing gender and caste boundaries.

To summarize, the image of India in the commentaries fluctuates between being beyond the scope of Christian imagination and being at its very center. These commentaries give an ambivalent picture, with India on the one hand portrayed as decadent and incapable of improving itself, and on the other hand as an amazing country overflowing with philosophers, poets, and wonderful people — philosophies "deep and subtle," classical literature "rich and extensive" (*Philippians* 20). Indian people, according to the commentators, were exploited, and these static masses were burdened and crushed by their own religions, philosophies, and way of life. Under such circumstances, the commentators put forward a strong case for British intervention and sought to incorporate Indians into the Western way of life through conversion.

Romans, Englishmen, and Indians

The commentaries employ subtle exegetical ploys to reinforce British intervention. One of the most striking is to point out similar outward characteristics between the Roman Empire and British rule. Acknowledging that conditions in British India are not perfectly analogous to those in the Roman Empire, the commentators detect at surface level at least three striking parallels regarding organization, peace, and culture.

Efficient administration is seen as the hallmark of Roman rule and the Roman political system, and this is attributed to the emperor and to the form of internal organization. Walker observes that just as power in the Roman Empire was vested in the emperor and the senate, so the British Raj is administered by the king-emperor and parliament. Just as the Roman Empire was divided into many provinces and also consisted of many client states, so the Indian portion of the British Empire consists of provinces such as Punjab, Bengal, and so forth, and also of native states such as Hyderabad, Travancore, and Mysore (*Acts* xxvii).

Second, Roman rule was presented as having brought peace, law,

and order. Internal strife and communal violence had given way to settled government. Similarly, the British presence in India was seen as
ushering in an era of peace and harmony. The following quotation,
from Walker, reinforces the view:

> For a century and a half after the death of Augustus, the empire
> enjoyed a period of almost unbroken peace. The strife of nations
> ceased within her borders. . . . Violent revolutions and civil commotions
> gave place to settled government and order. The various peoples who
> formed the subjects of the empire were glad to live quietly under the
> aegis of a strong and sovereign power. The "Pax Romana," or "Roman
> peace," gave security of life and property and ensured the regular ad-
> ministration of justice. Trade and commerce flourished. . . . It is easy to
> see in this a picture of the "Pax Britannica," the regime of peace and
> tranquillity which prevails under the British flag. With us, too, wars
> between race and race have given place to ordered rule. A unification
> of peoples and tribes is taking place such as India has never known
> before. (*Acts* xxviii)

The third parallel was with Roman culture. Just as the Greek language was seen as the language of scholarship and urbane manners,
so English is seen as fulfilling the same purposes in India. "[W]e
find the Anglo-Saxon tongue spoken by a rapidly increasing multitude throughout the length and breadth of India. And we, also, have
our Universities of Madras, Bombay, Allahabad from which a flowing
stream of English-speaking graduates in arts, philosophy, and science
issues forth year by year" (*Acts* xxxi). More important, the English
language is depicted as bringing together an imaginary unified people:
"As Greek bound together the peoples of the Roman empire, so English is more and more unifying the numerous races and peoples of this
great continent" (*Acts* xxxi).

In addition to these perceived parallels, there are a number of implicit exegetical allusions to similarities between Roman rule and the
British presence in India. Agrippa's visit to Caesarea to salute Fes-
tus (Acts 25:13) is interpreted as a native ruler paying formal respect
to a new viceroy or governor (*Acts* 522). Walker portrays Tertullus
(Acts 24:1) as one of the numerous Roman citizens who practice their
professions in the outposts of the Empire, just as many English barris-
ters carry on their practice in British India (*Acts* 501). To explain the
topography of Lycaonia — one of the districts that Paul visited, and
which had two parts, the east belonging to the native state of Anti-
ochus and the west to the Roman Empire — Walker compares it to the

state of Rajputana, which also had two parts, one of which was directly under British rule, the rest consisting of feudatory states (*Acts* 307).

Further, the British presence is consolidated by direct exegetical explication. Weitbrecht Stanton's reading of the tribute-money question (Matt. 22:15–22) is interesting. Where the Gospel writers see this incident as a climax in Jesus' confrontation with the religious and political authorities of his day, Weitbrecht Stanton ignores the political and confrontational tone of the narrative, and sees in Jesus' reply, "Render therefore unto Caesar the things that are Caesar's," a simple case of fair dealing. He goes on to write: "You profit by the protection and administration of the imperial government, and are willing to use [it to] enrich yourselves.... you are bound therefore to give back due value in the way of taxation for what you have received" (*Matthew* 554). In other words, Jesus is seen here as laying down the true relation of church to state: "[O]bedience to the secular authority in return for the benefits received, is a Christian duty" (*Matthew* 554). What we see here is the commentator making Jesus validate the Roman system, a system which was based on the conquest and subjugation of peoples.

The other interesting ploy is to invoke military images as a way of inculcating a feeling for the Empire. For instance, in exegeting Philippians 1:10, "that you may be sincere," Walker sees military connotations in the Greek origin of the word "sincere." Identifying three derivations of the word, he opts for the root meaning "a troop" or "a company," denoting "the orderly separateness of marshalled ranks," men standing shoulder to shoulder, but distinct from any motley crowd which may surround them. Then Walker extrapolates the significance of such a reading: "Here is a *thought for Christian Soldiers*, separate from the world, fighting the battles of their Lord. It appeals to us in India; we are among the heathen, but we must be separate from heathenism" (*Philippians* 39; italics in the original). Another case in point is Philippians 1:16: "I am set for the defense of the gospel." Walker, citing Bishop Moule, interprets the statement to mean like a soldier posted in the line of defense. He goes on to say that the image "would appeal to the Philippians as Roman citizens, 'placed' to defend the Empire on its outlying boundaries" (*Philippians* 44).

Such exegetical intervention clearly set out to legitimize the colonial presence of the British Empire. Waller in his commentary on the book of Revelation writes:

> In the days when the Revelation was written, the Empire had become
> firmly established and the people welcomed the reign of emperors as a

relief from the tyranny of the Old Roman Republican Governors whose chief thought had generally been to make money. Politically the change was similar to that which took place in India when the Governors-General were appointed in the place of the old Trading Company. The Roman law and administration gradually became paramount and crushed out much of the former civic activity. (*Revelation* 21)

Walker writes in a similar vein: "The Romans were noted for their organizing power and practical ability. They made great roads, established a settled peace, promoted facilities for trade and intercourse, carried everywhere a system of law and order, playing the part, in some respects, which Britain plays in the world to-day" (1911:100).

Though the commentators bring out the parallels between the Roman and British Empires, they also make it a point to discuss notable differences. Waller makes it clear that, unlike Roman rule, the current British administration did not encourage emperor worship, nor did it persecute Christians, and that it maintained neutrality on religious matters (*Revelation* 24). In the event that the Indians should read the Antichrist described in Revelation allegorically as the current king-emperor, Waller is quick to point out that the book clearly points to the future manifestation of the Antichrist and does not necessarily refer to historical figures (*Revelation* 266).

These commentaries present a picture of a Christianity which could not be identified with challenging or bringing down civil authorities. For these authors, the primary concern of the Christian faith is not the external condition but the inner soul of the individual. They gloss over the radical ideas of the Bible that would challenge the British presence in India. Instead, they inculcate the values of humility and obedience as exemplified in Jesus as a means to enjoying the benefits bestowed by British rule. Walker sums up the mood: "It was the Gospel which taught mankind that the way to true nobility of character is complete self-abnegation. We must learn of Christ the 'meek and lowly in heart,' if we would have true humility. This 'lowliness of mind' is the high road to all grace and blessing . . ." (*Philippians* 58).

These commentaries tried to demonstrate to the readers that the colonial British government was playing exactly the same role that the Romans had played. British rule was promoted as a modified and egalitarian incarnation of the Roman Empire, which held together under one administration different nationalities, languages, and customs. The Romans built roads, facilitated commerce, and conferred citizenship on all those they conquered. The result was that diverse groups of people were collapsed into one unified nation. The inference was that similar things were happening in India.

Concluding Observations

Taken as a whole, these commentarial texts testify to the triumphant complicity between evangelism and imperialism, but, in doing so, the writers unwittingly expose the contradictions of the Empire. While the commentaries proclaim the liberation that the gospel brings, the writers also replicate colonial attitudes and use rhetoric to redeem, educate, discipline, and convert the Indians who are under their charge. They become increasingly preoccupied with extolling the virtues of law, order, subservience, and authority supplied by the British Empire, seeing the Empire as a preparation for a greater human unity to be achieved through the legal and theological instruments of colonial power. They see their task as solidifying Christian faith and justifying the imperial power. The commentaries thus reveal the commentators' implication in the imperial project.

These commentaries were an early example of how a small band of people skillful in biblical criticism provided answers in a benevolent way, but made certain that those within their fold never asked awkward questions. The commentaries were silent about the political agitation and resistance fomenting in India at that time. They give the impression that British rule in India went unchallenged, and that it was India's good fortune to be governed by the British. The reading of the payment of tribute to Caesar in Matthew 22 bears this out. Glossing over the vexing political issues of the time, these commentaries offered Indians a simple choice between continuing their present life in misery and discontent, or in peace and with the prospect of a life of blessing in heaven. Walker wrote enthusiastically: "*They* live an earthly, grovelling life. Not so *we*. For *our* Metropolis is in heaven, and our aims and interests are centered there. We wait for a Savior to issue forth from that heavenly Homeland to take us to Himself" (*Philippians* 105, 106; italics and capitalization in original). These texts aimed to produce respectful and courteous Christians who would suffer patiently even under persecution (*Acts* 91). The commentators themselves were entrapped by the ideological codes of the time and, as a result, perverted their "gospel."

In a way, these commentaries serve as an early example of a bridge between biblical scholarship and the theological task. The commentators were pioneers in applied exegesis, engaged simultaneously in exegetical and theological work. Their endeavors would have received an approving nod from G. Ernest Wright, who wrote nearly four decades later: "We who are servants of the Church cannot be entirely dispassionate in our interpretation since we are actually committed to the Christian cause."[10] They freely actualized, though in some instances rather artificially, potential links between the two colonized worlds, first-century Palestine and twentieth-century India. They often abandon the cardinal rule of academic writing and employ the personal pronoun "I" as a more intimate way of discussing the interplay between theology and Scripture. They do not take a neutral stance, often resorting to the first-person plural and the liberal use of phrases like "Our Lord" and "Our Savior." The commentaries are full of exhortations such as "let us do this" and "let us avoid that." Though they worked within the modernist paradigm of detached, distanced, and objective reading, these writers went beyond it. They recognized that exegesis and exposition are committed, interested, and a positioned undertaking, a way of seeing the past in the light of present needs.

Superficially their approach may appear to resemble the current liberationist mode of seeking a synthesis between involvement and interpretation. Though their intentions may be similar, there is a vast difference between the missionary commentators and the practitioners of liberation hermeneutics. The difference lies in both the method and the goal. These commentaries were interventions premised on the belief in an objective truth, couched in ancient texts, which could be resituated in the Indian context regardless of differences of time, milieu, and culture, with a view to control and circumscribe Indians in power-loaded social relations. Current liberationists see the hermeneutical task the other way around. They start with an analysis of the given context of human poverty and oppression, and seek help from biblical texts by selecting and reappropriating them to suit their particular contextual concerns, with a view to empowering and raising the social consciousness of the people. Their goals, too, differ. For the missionary commentators the task was to rescue the sinner from damnation, whereas for the liberationist the aim is liberation in a much more comprehensive sense.

The significant achievement of these commentarial writings was to make modern European biblical scholarship available to Indian readers, but in the process authors tended to import its negative features as

---

10. I owe this quotation to Leander E. Keck. See his "The Premodern Bible in the Postmodern World," *Interpretation* 50, 2 (1996): 133.

well. One unsavory aspect was the introduction of anti-Semitism. Indians harbored hardly any anti-Semitic feeling. There have been contacts between the Jews and Indians since antiquity, with a number of small Jewish communities settled for some two thousand years, and these contacts have been marked by "absence of any hostility, persecution, and oppression" (Borowitz 1987:171). However, the commentaries unwittingly imported to India an exegetical practice which was part of European interpretative history. Many of the things the commentaries say about the relationship between the two testaments and the place of Judaism, and the anti-Semitic tone in their exegesis would not be accepted today. Indian readers were told that "Judaism was dying" at the time of Jesus (*2 Corinthians* 48) and that it was narrow and hard (*Hebrews* 46), a "religion of externalism" (*Philippians* 103); Moses was a "dead law-giver" (*2 Corinthians* 58), and "the Jews, who were prepared for 2000 years for the coming of Christ,... have been punished now for nearly 2000 years for their rejection of Him" (*John* 135).

Contrary to a missionary view that treated the Hebrew Scriptures as an outdated text, contemporary Hindu thinkers looked upon it favorably. Thus, they mobilized it to defend Hinduism against missionary attacks on their temple and worship practices. For instance, Arumuga Navalar (1822–79), a prominent Saiva reformer, saw the First Testament as endorsing worship practices similar to those of the Saiva community. He utilized his knowledge of the Old Testament "to show that far from being heathenish, the worship of Siva is fundamentally similar to the worship of God prescribed in the Old Testament, and followed by Jesus at the Temple in Jerusalem" (see Hudson 1994:55–56). As a way of delegitimizing the Christianity of the missionaries and contesting the nationalist criticism that all converts were allies of British colonialism, Arumainayagam, also known as Sattampillai (1824–1919), appropriated Jewish theological elements and restored them as the original and pure form of the Christian faith. The Church he started — The Hindu Christian Church of the Lord Jesus — was grounded in Jewish theology, and the place of worship he built for his followers was modeled on the Jerusalem Temple (Kumaradoss 1996:35–53; Thangaraj 1971:43–68). By relating their own location to the scriptural and cultural milieu of the Jews, Arumuga Navalar and Arumainayagam were not only able to affirm the potential value of their heritage, but also employed it as a potent means of resisting the colonizers. The evidence, on the other hand, of anti-Semitism that one finds in current Indian exegetical practice could well be attributed to the English commentaries, which bequeathed a perverse European phenomenon to the Indian Church.

The features of Indian society that these commentaries highlight, such as caste and corruption, were the standard missionary preoccupations of that time. This is not to deny that these features existed then or to suggest that they have subsequently vanished, but only to recognize that this emphasis served the imperial cause.

In constructing Christianity, these commentaries projected an idealized view of the Christian faith. Concepts such as love, justice, and equality are presented as the distinguishing marks of Christianity, overlooking its authoritative and repressive role in history. These commentators were untroubled by the fact that the very Bible they used to castigate the Indian caste system and superstition had been utilized on other occasions to support slavery, subordinate women, burn witches, and legitimize violation of other cultures.

Another element that we see in the commentaries is a group of missionaries coming to terms with a confusingly different culture, which seemed to threaten the stable categories and assumptions of their Christianity. Their difficulty was further exacerbated by their classical training, which failed to prepare them to meet religiously plural situations like India's. The commentaries in one sense operate on the same Eurocentric discursive continuum as travel literature, anthropology, popular novels, and cinema. The Empire remains largely unquestioned, and so does the cultural superiority of the West. These commentaries have all the hallmarks of colonialist literature. The echoes of Kipling on natives as "half-devil and half-child" permeate their pages. They were written by evangelical missionaries informed by theories of the superiority of European culture and the rightness of the Empire. Colonialism was not built on Christian values, but these were appropriated to justify the Empire. The commentators utilized the rhetoric of their writings to mediate the white man's relation to the natives. Put another way, these commentaries played their due part, along with the colonial administrators, educationalists, anthropologists, and so forth, in reinforcing the Raj.

Frantz Fanon said that colonialism was not simply content with firm control over the present and the future of a subjugated people, but needed to rewrite their past as well: "By a kind of perverted logic, it turns to the past of the oppressed people, and distorts, disfigures and destroys it" (1990:169). What these commentaries were trying to impress on their Indian readers was the unimportance of what had happened in precolonial days, before the arrival of the British. Their history, culture, and religions, the commentaries said, were dominated by superstition and barbarism. Christian faith and European learning brought the blessings of civilization. The benefits of the Empire were a means to a greater end. Christianity, often coupled with Western scientific knowledge and learning, was promoted as advantageous and indispensable to India's progress.

One of the legacies of these volumes was a series of hermeneutical practices and foreign thought patterns which effectively displaced indigenous ones. With these volumes and their like, biblical interpretation became a private, solitary activity. These commentaries helped to introduce the notion that interpretation is a literary activity limited to an educated, literate class, thus effectively replacing existing modes of oral transmission and communal connections. Interpretation in India used to be a public activity undertaken by groups of professional storytellers and singers who would travel to villages and narrate, chant, and recite religious stories and poems, often accompanied by musicians and dancers (Das 1991:36–38). Realizing the effectiveness of the method, the Indian Bible Society used to employ readers who would tour the villages to read the texts, and who would have face-to-face encounters with the local people.[11] For instance, an order of Bible Women would visit homes and villages and engage in biblical exposition. These women were more than interpreters. They acted as advisors, consultants, and solvers of all kinds of problems (Batley 132). Thus hermeneutics was not a private affair but a public one, in which villages would gather to hear the Word afresh, not necessarily through reading but by listening and interacting. These commentaries changed the mode of interpretation by replacing a group of listeners with a solitary reader, pursuing individual spiritual needs.

Finally, the Fanonian tripartite process — imitative, nativistic, and revolutionary — which the colonized go through in the face of colonialism, applies equally to the colonizers (Fanon 1990:178–79). Phebe Shih Chao, the Chinese cultural critic, sees this process among colonizers as first an acceptance and affirmation of colonialism, then as momentary guilt at its effects, and finally as a move to make amends (Chao 1997:292–93). Viewed in light of such categorizations, the missionary commentators fall within the first stage. In their hermeneutical practices they are strikingly unaware of the damage colonialism has

---

11. See W. A. Smith, "A Historical Study of the Protestant Use of the Bible for Evangelism in India" (M.R.S. thesis, Senate of Serampore, India, 1996), 52, 53.

done to other cultures. So engrossed in the task of Christianizing the natives, they almost overlooked the impact of colonialism.

In the televised version of Paul Scott's *The Jewel in Crown*, a British skeptic about the Empire describes the poverty and hunger evident on Calcutta's streets as "the legacy of all those blue-eyed Bible-thumpers who came out here because they couldn't stand the commercial pace back home." There were, of course, many progressive aspects to the impact of the West's mission in India, but these commentaries were too politically complacent to have much part in that. Essentially, the story of the Indian Church Commentaries is of "blue-eyed Bible-thumpers" who were more than satisfied with their own imperial perceptions.

Works Cited

I am extremely grateful to Dr. Dan O'Connor for drawing my attention to the existence of the Indian Church Commentaries and also for helping me to locate them, and to Suresh Kumar who generously photocopied several of them for me.

Appadurai, Arjun. 1988. "Putting Hierarchy in Its Place." *Cultural Anthropology* 3, 1:36–49.

Barker, Sir Ernest. 1995. "Some Constants of the English Character." In *Writing Englishness, 1900–1950: An Introductory Source Book on National Identity.* Ed. Judy Giles and Tim Middleton. London: Routledge, pp. 55–63.

Batley, D. S. n.d. *Devotees of Christ: Some Women Pioneers of the Indian Church.* London: Church of England Zenana Missionary Society.

Borowitz, Eugene B. 1987. "Judaism: An Overview." In *Encyclopedia of Religion.* Ed. M. Eliade. Vol. 8. New York: Macmillan.

Brown, E. F. 1923. *The First Epistle of Paul the Apostle to the Corinthians.* Madras: SPCK.

Chadwick, Owen. 1970. *The Victorian Church.* Part II. London: Adam & Charles Black.

Chao, Phebe Shih. 1997. "Reading *The Letter* in a Postcolonial World." In *Visions of the East: Orientalism in Film.* London: I. B. Tauris, pp. 292–313.

Crosthwaite, Arthur. 1916. *The Second Epistle to the Corinthians.* Madras: SPCK.

Das, Sisir Kumar. 1991. *A History of Indian Literature.* Vol. 8, *Western Impact: Indian Response, 1800–1910.* New Delhi: Sahitya Akademi.

Elliott-Binns, L. E. 1952. *The Development of English Theology in the Later Nineteenth Century.* London: Longmans, Green, and Co.

Fanon, Frantz. [1961] 1990. *The Wretched of the Earth.* Harmondsworth: Penguin Books.

Firminger, Walter Kelly. 1921. *The Epistles of St. Paul the Apostle to the Colossians and to Philemon.* Madras: SPCK.

Gramsci, Antonio. 1976. *Selections from the Prison Notebooks of Antonio Gramsci.* Ed. Quintin Hoare and Geoffrey Nowell Smith. London: Lawrence and Wishart.

Holmes, W. H. G. 1929. *The Epistle to the Hebrews.* Madras: SPCK.

Hudson, Dennis D. 1994. "A Hindu Response to the Written Torah." In *Between Jerusalem and Benares: Comparative Study in Judaism and Hinduism.* Ed. Hananya Goodman. Albany: State University of New York Press, pp. 55–84

Kumaradoss, Vincent. 1996. "Negotiating Colonial Christianity: The Hindu Christian Church of Late Nineteen Century Tirunelveli." *South Indian Studies* 1:35–53.

Lightfoot, J. B. 1896. *Historical Essays.* London: Macmillan.

Neill, Stephen, and Tom Wright. 1988. *The Interpretation of the New Testament, 1861–1986.* Oxford: Oxford University Press.

Pakenham-Walsh, H. 1921. *The Epistles of St. John.* Madras: SPCK.

Pals, Daniel L. 1982. *The Victorian "Lives" of Jesus.* San Antonio: Trinity University Press.

Said, Edward W. [1978] 1985. *Orientalism.* Harmondsworth: Penguin Books.

Stanton, Weitbrecht. 1919. *The Gospel according to St. Matthew.* Madras: SPCK.

Thangaraj, Thomas M. 1971. "The History and Teachings of the Hindu-Christian Community Called Nattu Sabai in Tirunelveli." *The Indian Church History Review* 5, 1:43–68.

Walker, T. 1906. *The Epistle to the Philippians.* Madras: SPCK.

———. 1911. *Missionary Ideals: Missionary Studies in the Acts of the Apostles.* London: Church Missionary Society.

———. 1919. *The Acts of the Apostles.* Madras: SPCK.

Waller, E. H. M. 1926. *The Revelation of St. John the Divine.* Madras: SPCK.

Westcott, Brooke Foss. 1873. *On Some Points in the Religious Office of the Universities.* London: Macmillan.

———. 1897. *Christian Aspects of Life.* London: Macmillan.

4

Textual Cleansing

From a Colonial to a Postcolonial Version

I, too, am a translated man.... It is generally believed that some-
thing is always lost in translations; ... I cling to the notion that
something can also be gained. —SALMAN RUSHDIE in *Shame*

I put my tales of you into lasting songs. The secret gushes out
from my heart. They come and ask me, "Tell me all your mean-
ings." I know not how to answer them. I say, "Ah, who knows
what they mean!" They smile and go away in utter scorn. And
you sit there smiling. —RABINDRANATH TAGORE in *Gitanjali*

In this chapter I attempt to do the following: (*a*) to look at the translation strategies and practices of the colonial period, and to map out how
these literary outputs abetted and reflected the racial and class bias of
the colonizer; (*b*) to look at the effects of these translation enterprises
on Indians; and (*c*) to move a step further and make proposals for a
wider intertextual reading, and a postcolonial version of translation.
In looking at the colonial period, my intention is not to scrutinize the
translations as such but to investigate motives and presuppositions as
they are outlined in the translators' prefaces and introductions.[1] During
the colonial period three groups of translators took an active interest —
Orientalists, missionaries, and civil administrators. Each in his/her
own way was trying to make available the Christian Scriptures in vernacular languages and was also trying to translate indigenous texts into

---

1. For an investigation into the nature, scope, and suitability of postcolonialism, from
a variety of perspectives, see Mongia 1996; Barker, Hulme, and Iversen 1994; Trivedi and
Mukherjee 1996; Williams and Chrisman 1993; Ashcroft, Griffiths, and Tiffin 1989.

European languages. Such intelligible and unambiguous literary production assumed the tone that translation was a one-way flow from a superior race to an inferior one, and aimed at the moral and intellectual improvement of the natives. It also helped in fixing the texts of the colonized as decadent and in need of purification. William Carey, a Baptist missionary who was at the forefront of translation activity in India during the colonial period, sums up the mood: "The advantage of being able to communicate useful knowledge to the heathens, with whom we have a daily intercourse; to point out their mistakes; and impress upon them sentiment of morality and religion, are confessedly very important" (1818:vi).

Imperial Race, Mercantile Class:
Creating the Difference

The great translation activities were undertaken during what scholars characterize as the "Orientalist" and "Anglicist" phases of the colonial history of India. Orientalists pursued a policy of promoting Sanskrit literature, philosophy, and court culture, whereas Anglicists were vigorous in propagating Western education and values. Both Orientalists and Anglicists had an ambivalent attitude toward India's ancient traditions. On the one hand, they had the scholarly and the natural urge to unlock this ancient and mysterious wisdom. On the other hand, they were under a colonial compulsion to expose India's glorious past as superstitious, stagnant, abased, and degenerate, and then to use this as an argument for foreign intervention and the introduction of Christianity. Though Orientalist and Anglicist phases emerged out of different ideological and colonial needs, they basically agreed on the following:·

1. Indian texts are defiled and are in need of theological cleansing. William Ward, one of the Serampore triumvirate (in addition to the aforementioned William Carey and Joshua Marshman), in his preface to *A View of the History, Literature, and Mythology of the Hindus*, writes: "Multitudes of fables and scenes are found in the most chaste of the Hindoo writings, belonging to the histories of their gods and ancient sages, that are disgusting beyond all utterance..." (1820:xxxviii).

2. Native interpreters are unreliable. William Carey encouraged imperial administrators and company servants to transact business and to "inspect all the minutiae of mercantile concerns, without the intervention of an interpreter," because overreliance on local interpreters may

restrict their "free conversation with all classes of people." He warned them that to "go through the medium of servants...would not only be liable to innumerable impositions" but also would be "frequently rendered abortive by the ignorance or inattention of those to whom the management thereof is committed" (1818:iii, vi).

3. The colonizer has an inalienable right to explain and speak on behalf of the natives. These discourses desire to produce a manageable "Other," and to show the subjects how to maintain and behave themselves. What Roland Inden said of Orientalists applies equally to the translators as well: "[They have] appropriated the power to represent the Oriental, to translate and explain his [and her] thoughts and acts not only to Europeans and Americans but also to the Orientals themselves. But this is not all. Once his special knowledge enabled the Orientalist and his countrymen to gain trade concessions, conquer, colonize, rule, and punish in the East" (1986:408). The translation efforts denied a voice to the colonized but allowed a form of behavior based on the images fabricated and nurtured by the colonizer. Translation, thus, is more than a mere linguistic enterprise. It is a site for promoting unequal relationships among languages, races, religions, and peoples. It brings into focus the manipulative position of a translator.

Two key aspects of colonial translations are the representation of the Other and the production of knowledge. In representing particular versions of the colonialized, translators were able to project themselves as the superior race and to embody class positions which paved the way for the stabilization of the British rule and for the introduction of the Bible and Christian way of life. Such a notion of racial superiority was undergirded by a progressive, evolutionary notion of history. In this idea of history, textual tradition, religious practices, and behavioral patterns of the colonized were distorted and perceived as an immature version of what could be found in normal Western society. This view of history places European races at the pinnacle of civilization and relegates the colonized to a subservient and subject position. In other words, colonial translations justified the colonizer's civilizing mission, and established the inherent superiority of the colonizer's culture.

One of the ploys used to maintain racial superiority was to demonize the Other and to emphasize racial, gender, and class differences. Missionaries promulgated descriptions of Hindus as barbaric, submissive, ignorant, intellectually "far lower than that of our ancestors" (Ward 1820:lii), irrational, and possessing "no powers, except those of the animal" (xxxiv). Valorization of these differences allowed the imperialists to subjugate Indians and also to perceive themselves as beneficent agents of God's will. Ward declares that the "mental and moral improvement" of India is the "high destiny" of the British nation and also its "national glory" which "will eclipse all her other achievements" (liv). He proudly claimed that "Great Britain is the only country upon earth, from which the intellectual and moral improvement of India could have been expected" (xvii). The following two testimonies bear witness to the civilizing effects. A missionary from South India wrote:

> The moral conduct, upright dealing, and decent dress, of the native Protestants of Tanjore, demonstrate the powerful influence and peculiar excellence of the Christian religion. It ought, however, to be observed that the Bible, when the reading of it becomes general, has nearly the same effect on the poor of every place. (Quoted in Zemka 1991: 131–32)

Similarly, Robert Moffat from South Africa wrote of the civilizing nature his translation of Luke had on the people of Botswana: "[T]hus, by the slow but certain progress of Gospel principles, whole families became clothed and in their right mind" (quoted in Zemka 1991:132). Thus the vested interest in interiorizing Hindus was to make them realize that their salvation lay in conversion to the religion of a superior people.

Missionary translators also helped in producing and creating a consumer class. Most of the missionaries were dissenters and marginalized citizens in their own country, but once in the colonies they identified themselves with the English state and became spokespersons for the mercantile class of the time. They took upon themselves the task of perpetuating the class interest of the rulers and the capitalist intentions of the company. Grammars, dictionaries, and lexicons were produced by the missionaries as a way of acquainting the company servants and civil administrators with a working knowledge of the languages, so that colonial rulers could administer justice and collect revenues (Carey 1818:vi). Missionary translators also saw their task as introducing consumer values and the interest of the mercantile class to Indians. Ward lamented the "extraordinary fact" that the British goods purchased annually by India were "not sufficient to freight a single vessel from our ports." But he maintained that once Indians were enlightened and civilized they could "contribute more to the real prosperity of Britain as a commercial people by consuming her manufactures to a vast extent." He went on to write:

But let Hindost'han receive that higher civilization she needs, that cultivation of which she is so capable; let European literature be transfused into all her languages, then the ocean, from the ports of Britain to India, will be covered with our merchant vessels; and from the center of India moral culture and science will be extended all over Asia, to the Burman empire and Siam, to China, with all her millions, to Persia, even to Arabia....(1820:liii)

Thus the missionary translators' desire to produce an entrepreneurial mercantile class proved increasingly suited to the capitalist interests of the company.

Effects of the Translations

The enormous amount of translation undertaken by missionaries had a profound impact on the colonized. Briefly I identify the following:

1. Semitization. By privileging the Bible as the sacred text embodying the religious identity of the people, the missionaries introduced a concept alien to Hindus — a fixed holy text which acted as an objective marker of a religious community. Hindu attitudes to religious texts have been marked by a high degree of dynamism and fluidity. The imposition under colonial and missionary pressure of a Semitic understanding of sacred works and Scriptures forced Hindus to come up with their own versions of the holy book. They came to believe the *Bhagavad Gita* the Hindu text worthy to be placed along with the Christian Bible. Bhikhu Parekh, an Indian political theorist, writes:

Once the British consolidated their rule and used all the resources of the state to denigrate Hinduism, Hindus lost their self-confidence and many of them began to mimic Christianity. They turned Krishna into their equivalent of Christ, singled out the Gita as their Bible...created Church-like organization in the form of the Ramakrishna Mission and Arya Samaj, and so on. (1989:8)

Such Semitization of Hindu faith, according to Parekh, led to the loss of its authenticity and seriously weakened its fabric. While people had paid little attention to written texts but preserved their sacred contents through rigorous memorization and recitation, the missionary influence led them to defer to written authority. During the colonial rule, Hindu reformers called constantly for a revival based on ancient and authoritative texts like the *Vedas* and the *Upanishads.* The near-canonical status the *Gita* attained during the freedom struggle is another case in point. Those who resisted the colonial rule, freedom fighters like Gandhi, Aurobindo, Vinoba Bhave, and Radhakrishnan, looked to the *Gita* for a philosophy of action, and went on to produce commentaries. The primacy they accorded a written text is underlined in Gandhi's words: "What, however, I have done is to put a new but natural and logical interpretation upon the whole teaching of the Gita and the spirit of Hinduism. Hinduism, not to speak of other religions, is ever-evolving. It has not one Scripture like the Quran or the Bible. Its Scriptures are also evolving and suffering addition. The Gita itself is an instance in point. It has given a new meaning to *karma, sannyasa, yajna,* and so forth. It has breathed a new life into Hinduism" (quoted in Dalton 1982:8). The Hindus' elevation of the written text over the oral is the by-product of the missionary translation enterprise.

By privileging the written texts as the valid medium for sacred communication, missionary translations devalued the orality and rhetoric of hearing. In trying to render word for word, translators failed to take note of the function the words had in Indian thinking. Bernard Cohn points out the different Indian and English perceptions of language:

> Meaning for the English was something attributed to a word, a phrase or an object, which could be determined and translated, hopefully with a synonym which had a direct referent to something in what the English thought of as a "natural" world. Everything had a more or less specific referent for the English. With the Indians, meaning was not necessarily construed in the same fashion. The effect and affect of hearing a Brahmin chanting in Sanskrit at a sacrifice did not entail meaning in the European sense; it was to have one's substance literally affected by the sound. (1990:279)

2. The Bible translations in the colonial period introduced such virtues as accuracy, authenticity, and being true to original texts — virtues to which Indian translators paid less attention. Indians were more interested in the aesthetic flavor than literal accuracy. Ayyappa Paniker, the Indian literary critic, poet, and translator, reckons that the attempts to translate the Bible into Indian languages introduced the problematic question of authenticity (1994:130). The nineteenth-century Indian translators were not unduly worried about being true to the original version. Countless vernacular versions of classical Sanskrit works, epics, and puranas have been produced, rewritten, retold, modified, and subverted by Indians without paying much attention to accuracy. When Kamban, the Tamil poet, produced Valmiki's *Ra-*

mayana in Tamil, he took all the freedom he needed to make it his own version, and turned it into a Tamil classic. What was paramount for Indian translators was the poetic features of the language into which a text was translated, and the aesthetic tastes of the readers/hearers at whom the translations were aimed. In commenting on the practices of Indian medieval translators, Paniker writes:

> The impression one gets from all these multiple versions is that, not only was literal adherence to the original not insisted on, but that deviation was liberally tolerated, even encouraged and preferred.... The poetics of medieval Indian translations could perhaps be understood and interpreted in terms of the visible absence of the anxiety of authenticity on the part of these "translators." If the local/regional versions of *Ramayana* and *Mahabharata* became the classics of the regional literatures, the reason is not far to seek. These adapted translations were well received by the public in each region. There was nothing "alien" about them. (1994:129–30)

Toward a Postcolonial Translation Strategy

Finally, in the last part of the chapter, I would like to propose a different translation strategy in a changed context. First, in a postcolonial, postmissionary era, translation should seek for a wider intertextuality which will link biblical texts with Asian scriptural texts. In other words, if we wish to take the religious texts of Asians seriously, we need to go beyond the missionaries' attempt to purify these texts to illuminating the Christian texts with the help of indigenous religious texts. Second, at a point in our history when we have different versions of the Bible to cater to different ecumenical, gender, and denominational needs, the time has come for a version which will reflect postcoloniality and will take into account postcolonial English. In a postcolonial context, translation does not mean retrieving an original purity or striving for linguistic nicety, but radically reinscribing and, in the process, radically disrupting the text.

"Postcolonial" is a contested term. The question of its usefulness and validity has enlisted vigorous debate among those at different institutions. The debate centers around, among other things, whether postcolonialism is about a state, condition, or a critical reading strategy. Postcolonialism is not about a mere periodization; it is a reading posture, emerging from the colonized Other. It is a critical enterprise aimed at unmasking the link between ideas and power which lies behind Western theories and learning. It is a discursive resistance against imperialism, imperial ideologies, imperial attitudes, and their continued incarnations among such wide-ranging fields as politics, economics, and history, and theological and biblical studies.

A Wider Textual Interweaving

A wider intertextual reading will link biblical texts with Asian scriptural texts. Intertextuality means looking for — besides racism, sexism, and classism — what John Hull calls "religionism" in the text and in the subsequent translations of the texts. Hull defines it thus:

> Religionism describes an adherence to a particular religion which involves the identity of the adherent so as to support tribalistic or nationalistic solidarity. The identity which is fostered by religionism depends upon rejection and exclusion. We are better than they. We are orthodox; they are infidel. We are believers; they are unbelievers. We are right; they are wrong. The other is identified as the pagan, the heathen, the alien, the stranger, the invader, the one who threatens us and our way of life. (1992:70)

Religionism is a form of religion in which the individual and collective identity of one religious group is maintained by asserting negative aspects of the other. In the colonial context missionaries asserted the primacy of Christian faith by highlighting gloomy aspects of other faith traditions. Colonial and missionary translators maintained and believed in Christianity as the only valid religion and a sure route to God. Their translations helped in the proselytizing process and thereby attempted to erase the existence of other religions.

The rethinking of the translation in the postcolonial context becomes important when the hitherto-held "master narrative" is read alongside other equally life-affirming narratives offered by other religious communities. Establishing correct textual and conceptual affinities between Christian texts and other Hindu, Buddhist, and Confucian writings may not be easy. However, George Soares-Prabhu, the Indian biblical scholar, has attempted to compare Buddhist and Christian texts despite the fact that both emerge from two different chronological, literary, and theological contexts. He reckons the appropriate way to read the Bible in a religiously pluralistic context like Asia is to create a matrix of biblical narratives and Asia's sacred texts. As an example, he has done a comparative hermeneutical study of Jesus' missionary command in Matthew (28:16–20) with the command Buddha gave to his followers, as narrated in the *Mahavagga* 11.1, a section of the Vinaya text of the Pali canon.

This will lead to an Asian theology of liberation emerging not from the Bible alone but also from the stories and texts of Asian religions that are read with it. . . . Here, it is the reading of the Bible that must be illustrated by the Asian religious texts and stories which are brought to it, so that it begins to reveal the biblical way to the "disinterested action" (*nishkama karma*) of the Bhagavadgita (2.47; 4.18–20), or to that unshakable "calm" (*santam*), like that of a deep lake clear and still, which in the Dhammapada (6.7; 7.7) is the mark of the "saint" (*arhant*). For without such spiritual freedom, attempts at other kinds of liberation will inevitably end in further bondage. The "enlightenment" of Kant must be completed by the enlightenment of the Buddha, the liberation of Marx with the "liberation" of the Gita. It is to achieve a dialectical interplay of these three freedoms that we attempt Asian interpretations of the Bible, by relating it to Asian stories and Asian texts. (1994:273–74)

Soares-Prabhu's study demonstrates that such wider intertextual study helps us to arrive "at a more rounded interpretation of the mission command in Matthew, by pointing to elements implicit in it, which, though explicit elsewhere in the Gospel, could be overlooked in an over-focused, atomistic reading of the text" (1994:282). Such an intertextual hermeneutics could illuminate many gaps and silences in the biblical texts, and brighten some dark corners.

A Postcolonial Version?

The numerous versions of English translations currently available on the market are generally dismissive of the postcolonial contexts and claim a universal validity for Anglo-American English. These versions fail to take note of the emergence of English outside the native Anglo-Saxon milieu. The recent emergence of postcolonial literature has given birth to English with a distinctive flavor. Rather than mimicking or appropriating the metropolitan model, commonwealth writers such as Salman Rushdie, Arundhati Roy, Vikram Seth, Chinua Achebe, and Ngugi wa Thiong'o have not only decolonized English but have re-created it, infusing native perceptions, metaphors, similes, experiences, and speech patterns. In their writings, English is deterritorialized out of its "classical frontiers." It is taken out of its metropolitan control and ingrafted with vernacular idioms, syntax, and poetics. For instance, the following quote from Rushdie's recent novel, *The Moor's Last Sigh* (1995), illustrates how verbal "conjoining" celebrates hybridity and multiculturalism. Moraes Zogoiby, a crossbreed himself, is the novel's narrator. He chronicles the ups and downs of four generations of his family and describes himself thus: "I, however, was raised neither as Catholic nor as Jew. I was both, and nothing: a jewholic-anonymous, a cathjew nut, a stewpot, a mongrel cur. I was — what's the word these days? — *atomised*. Yessir: a real Bombay mix" (1995:104; italics in the original). The novel sparkles with similar funny language which is familiar to generations of English-speaking Indians.

Another example of how English language has been dexterously and alluringly ambushed, or recolonized, occurs in the work of Ken Saro-wiwa, the Nigerian novelist and human rights activist who was put to death by his own government for trying to find redress for his Ogoni people. The subtitle of his novel, *Sozaboy: A Novel in Rotten English* (1994), gives a clue to the authorial intention.

> Sozaboy's language is what I call "rotten English," a mixture of Nigerian pidgin English, broken English and occasional flashes of good, even idiomatic English. The language is disordered and disorderly. Born of a mediocre education and severely limited opportunities, it borrows words, patterns and images freely from the mother-tongue and finds expression in a very limited English vocabulary. To its speakers, it has the advantage of having no rules and no syntax. It thrives on lawlessness, and is part of the dislocated and discordant society in which Sozaboy must live, move and have not his being. (1994:author's note)

K. Satchidanandan, the Indian literary critic, writes of the post-colonized English:

> English, in this context, is decolonized through a nativisation of theme, space and time, a change of canon from the Western to the Indian, a cohesive use of the discoursal devices of other languages of the writer — like native metaphors, similes, proverbs, quotations, speech-acts, culturally appropriate styles — even transliteration of conversions done in the Indian language.... (1995:6)

What we aim for is a version of the Bible which will take into account the postcolonial English and mobilize it radically to rewrite the text, to soak it with new angles and new perspective. What Harish Trivedi, the Indian cultural critic, said in another context is equally applicable to biblical translations:

> [D]o we as translators at all need to strive to attain an alien, transatlantic idiom? Would it not then be more effective to retain as much of the original tone, idiom and sensibility as we could, and to deploy for the purpose our own ethnically and linguistically marked

and flavoursome "Indian" English? Had not the distinctly successful younger generation of our Indo-Anglian writers, who had risen in the wake of Rushdie's Booker, actually foregrounded and exploited an implicit bilingualism in their use of English? Had they not "chutnified" the language as well as history.... (1994:126)

In the pickling of chutney, what is decomposable is conserved through a process which adds a new taste and color. Chutnification acts as an apt metaphor for rewriting and retranslating, and, in effect, for spicing up the text. To the chutnification of language and history, I would like to add biblical narratives. What the postcolonial translation will attempt is to select and rewrite biblical narratives, and in doing so will not only rid them of their ideological trappings and contest received interpretations, but also inject them with new flavor and taste. For instance, it will retell the parable of the prodigal son, not from the father's perspective, perceiving him as a benevolent patriarch, but from the point of view of the son, seeing the father as one who refuses to grant his son's individuality and delights in his failure. At a time when Asian family values are extolled as superior, and Asian discipline and industriousness are paraded as supreme examples to be emulated, it is time for sons and daughters of Asia, who often suffocate under its stranglehold, to seek for freedom and individuality by retranslating the parable which resonates with their plight. Thomas Palakeel, the Indian author, brings out this aspect poignantly in his short story, "The Serpent and the Master" (1994), a reworking of the prodigal son. In this story the son attempts to escape the dominance of the father, his parental control, and the pressures of the extended family to lead a life of his own choosing. After realizing that dreams alone are not adequate to see him through the world, the son returns home. The reception he receives gives the clue to the story and the angle from which it has been approached:

> My family celebrated when I came back. It was a rainy evening. The last rain of the season. I stepped onto the verandah. Father saw me first. He did not move for a moment; he got up, very slowly. Then he exclaimed: "Bring tea for Appu. Look who's come back. He's back. Oh, God."
>
> I detested the frantic joy on my father's face. Fathers always rejoice when their prodigal sons return home, defeated. A father waits for the son's fall. (182)

Translation in a postcolonial context is not merely seeking dynamic equivalence or aiming for linguistic exactness, but desires to rewrite and retranslate the texts, as well as the concepts, against the grain. Rewriting and retranslating are not a simple dependence upon the past, but a radical remolding of the text to meet new situations and demands.

Let me end with an actual incident from colonial times. It describes aptly the tension generated between colonized and colonizer when faced with contested translations, and how stereotypical images are shattered. Claudius Buchanan, a provost at Fort William College, Calcutta, a college which trained the colonial administrators, was in his paternalistic benevolent way trying to impose a standard translation of the Malayalam Bible on the Malayalees, and proposed that they should copy it and circulate it among themselves. To this proposal, one of the elders, Thomas or Didymus, replied: "To convince you, Sir, of our earnest desire to have the Bible in Malayalam tongue, I need only mention that I have lately translated the gospel of St. Matthew for the benefit of my children. It is often borrowed by the other families. It is not in fine language, but the people love to read it." A Malayali priest listening in commented: "But how shall we know that your standard copy is a true translation of our Bible? We cannot depart from our own Bible. It is the true word of God, without corruption — that book used by the Christians at Antioch. What translations you have got in the West, we do not know: But the true Bible of Antioch we have had in the mountains of Malabar for fourteen hundred years, or longer. Some of our copies are from ancient times; so old and decayed, that they can scarce be preserved much longer" (Buchanan 1840:25).

The answers challenge not only the stereotypical image of a native as a mute, incompetent, and hapless person, but also reframe him or her as a human being with perception and competence. The colonized disconcerted the colonizer not only by not incorporating hegemonic interpretations and values, but also by demonstrating that they, the colonized, had knowledge and power. Subalterns did speak and they will continue to speak.

Works Cited

Ashcroft, Bill, Gareth Griffiths, and Helen Tiffin, eds. 1989. *The Empire Writes Back: Theory and Practice in Post-colonial Literatures*. London: Routledge.

——. 1995. *The Post-colonial Studies Reader*. London: Routledge.

Barker, Francis, Peter Hulme, and Margaret Iversen, eds. 1994. *Colonial Discourse/Postcolonial Theory*. Manchester: Manchester University Press.

Buchanan, Claudius. 1840. *Christian Researches in India*. London: SPCK.

Carey, William. 1818. *A Grammar of the Bengalee Language.* Fourth edition with additions. Serampore: Mission Press.

Cohn, Bernard S. [1985] 1990. "The Command of Language and the Language of Command." In *Subaltern Studies IV: Writings on South Asian History and Society.* Ed. Ranajit Guha. Delhi: Oxford University Press, pp. 276–329.

Dalton, Dennis G. 1982. *Indian Idea of Freedom: Political Thought of Swami Vivekananda, Aurobindo Ghose, Mahatma Gandhi, and Rabindranath Tagore.* Gurgaon: Academic Press.

Hull, John. 1992. "The Transmission of Religious Prejudice." *British Journal of Religious Education* 14, 2:69–72

Inden, Roland. 1986. "Orientalist Constructions of India." *Modern Asian Studies* 20, 3:401–46.

Mongia, Padmini. 1996. *Contemporary Postcolonial Theory: A Reader.* London: Arnold.

Palakeel, Thomas. 1994. "The Serpent and the Master." *Yatra: Writing from the Indian Subcontinent* 4:171–82.

Paniker, Ayyappa K. 1994. "The Anxiety of Authenticity: Reflections on Literary Translation." *Indian Literature* 37, 4:128–38.

Parekh, Bhikhu. 1989. "The Concept of Inter-faith Dialogue." *Faith and Freedom* 42, 124 (Spring): 5–12.

Saro-wiwa, Ken. 1994. *Sozaboy: A Novel in Rotten English.* Harlow: Longman.

Satchidanandan, K. 1995. "On Indian Writing in English." *Indian Literature* 38, 3:5–8.

Soares-Prabhu, George M. 1994. "Two Mission Commands: An Interpretation of Matthew 28:16–20 in the Light of a Buddhist Text." *Biblical Interpretation: A Journal of Contemporary Approaches* 2, 3:264–82.

Rushdie, Salman. 1995. *The Moor's Last Sigh.* London: Jonathan Cape.

Trivedi, Harish. 1994. "Translating Together for Home and Abroad: An Experiment and an Experience." *Indian Literature* 37, 4:109–27.

Trivedi, Harish, and Meenakshi Mukherjee, eds. 1996. *Interrogating Postcolonialism: Theory, Text, and Context.* Shimla: Indian Institute of Advanced Study.

Ward, William. 1820. *A View of the History, Literature, and Mythology of the Hindus: Including a Minute Description of Their Manners and Customs and Translations from Their Principal Work.* Vol. 3. London: Black, Kingsbury, Parbury, and Allen.

Williams, Patrick, and Laura Chrisman, eds. 1993. *Colonial Discourse and Post-colonial Theory: A Reader.* New York: Harvester Wheatsheaf.

Zemka, Sue. 1991. "The Holy Books of Empire: Translations of the British and Foreign Bible Society." In *Macropolitics of Nineteenth-Century Literature: Nationalism, Exoticism, Imperialism.* Ed. Jonathan Arac and Harriet Ritvo. Philadelphia: University of Pennsylvania Press, pp. 102–37.

Part II

ORIENTALISM AND BIBLICAL SCHOLARSHIP

5

Orientalism, Ethnonationalism, and Transnationalism
Shifting Identities and Biblical Interpretation

We need no longer offer explanations. . . . It matters not whether we are good or bad, civilized or barbarian, so long as we are but ourselves. —RABINDRANATH TAGORE in *Gora*

"Actually, we're all possessed by cultural otherness in one way or another, aren't we?" he asked.

"Except, at this moment in time it can be sort of hard to say what makes for a cultural self and what's an other. . . . People like us are this impossible collage, aren't we?"

"Tell me about it!" Firoze shouted back.

. . . "You know," Gita reflected, "When I first came here I used to see everything in terms of dichotomies: America was this big lonely place, and so when I thought of India it was mostly in terms of happy things. I also used to think there was a space I could arrive where I'd understand everything and be contented ever after."

"But when you got older, and you saw that everything is mixed up, every horizon opens onto another even more complicated one, and no solution is ever final," said Firoze.

"Exactly," said Gita.

—KIRIN NARAYAN in *Love, Stars, and All That*

It is becoming increasingly clear that nationalities, self-identities, and cultures are constructed in response to the "Other." Edward Said has been instrumental in initiating a lively academic interest in what has now come to be known as colonial discourse studies. His *Orientalism* (1985) focuses on how, in a variety of ways, the West has been able to produce texts and codify knowledge about the Other, especially in the form of those who were under its colonial control. He defines Orientalism as dealing with the Orient "by making statements about it, authorizing views of it, describing it, by teaching it, settling it, ruling over it: in short, Orientalism as a Western style for dominating, restructuring, and having authority over the Orient" (1985:3). In his view, it is a systematic discipline "by which European culture was able to manage — even produce — the Orient politically, sociologically, militarily, ideologically, scientifically, and imaginatively during the post-Enlightenment period" (1985:3). In other words, Orientalism results in not just a textualizing of the Orient, but a textualizing on behalf of and as a representation of the Orient, thus making it amenable to certain kinds of control and manipulation. In effect, what Orientalism achieved was that "European culture gained in strength and identity by setting itself off against the Orient as a sort of surrogate and even underground self" (1985:3). In characterizing and defining the Other, the West characterized and defined itself — as a superior culture "in comparison with all the non-European peoples and cultures" (1985:7). Inevitably, Said's thesis elicited a great amount of controversy and interest among both Western and postcolonial intellectuals. As a consequence of the debate, Said himself has gone on to address some of the criticism and to widen his focus to explore the lasting legacy of colonialism — its cultural and intellectual control (*Culture and Imperialism,* 1993).

Said's thesis mainly concerns European attitudes to western Asia and Islam, and has no direct relevance to biblical materials, though he points out that during the early nineteenth century the Orient meant only India and the Bible lands (1985:4). This present essay engages Said's thesis, highlighting the traces of Orientalist ideas, habits, and categories in biblical scholarship, and how both Western and third world scholars have made use of Orientalistic formulae to define their identities. It tries to move the debate a step further by discussing the role of the biblical interpreter at a time when national identities, geographical borders, and cultural boundaries are being redrawn, remapped, and redesigned.

Oriental Mannerisms, Biblical Interpreters

One can often identify signs of Orientalism in the writings of biblical scholars. As a way of illustrating this I would like to use the works of Joachim Jeremias, and especially his *The Parables of Jesus* (1963) — a near-classic in which countless third world biblical scholars were schooled. Several of the exegetical conclusions at which Jeremias arrives betray his Eurocentric perception of the Other. The negative caricatures of the characters, the condescending remarks he makes about the narrative style of indigenous storytellers, and the stereotyping of the landscape are all akin to the travel writing, novels, and other literary productions of the colonial era, rather than to the marks of a serious biblical scholarship which professes to be rooted in objective science. For him the East is hot (1963:140) and full of beggars (159); people go to bed early (157); women are fertile, inferior, and submissive (1969:375); the rich are brutal (1963:195); and storytellers exaggerate and hype their materials. For instance, in the parable of the talents, when Matthew boosted the amount of money and Luke increased the number of servants, Jeremias attributes this hype to the Oriental storyteller's penchant for large numbers, which "led to embellishment in both versions of the story" (1963:28). Similarly, the fruitful harvest in the parable of the sower is dismissed as "abnormal tripling, after the oriental fashion" (1963:150). Even Jesus does not escape Jeremias's Eurocentric jibes. The inflated contract figures in Luke 16:1–9 are dismissed as "the oriental story-teller's love for large numbers" (1963:181).

The Parables also perpetuates the notion of the Other as lazy and unreliable. When commenting on the parable of the laborers in the vineyard (Matt. 20:1–16), he states that the excuse of the laborers who were hanging around, that no one had hired them, was their "cover for their typical oriental indifference" (1963:37, 137). Such exegetical comments are based not so much on the economic realities of the time, or the employment opportunities available to the laborers, as on the Eurocentric view of the Oriental as a lazy native.

Look again at his comments on the parable of the wicked servant (Luke 16:1–9). When the steward adjusts the accounts of the debtors, Jeremias's reaction is very interesting. He attributes the extraordinary behavior of the steward to the people in the East not knowing anything of bookkeeping or audits (1963:181). At one stroke, he not only elevates European achievements in accounting but also rules out the contributions the Chinese, Indians, and Egyptians have made toward the development of present-day mathematics — a point cogently argued by George Gheverghese Joseph in his recent book, *The Crest of the Peacock: Non-European Roots of Mathematics* (1991). Such a claim also demonstrates the Eurocentric parochialism of Jeremias, which denies the possibility of other people having different ways of accounting. The exegetical comment on the same parable by Margaret Gibson during the height of the colonial period is worth recalling. Her considered view was that the behavior of the steward was a custom that prevailed "whenever Orientals are left to their own methods, uncontrolled by any protectorate of Europeans" (1902/3:334).

Jeremias also reinscribes the nineteenth-century binary typology which posited that there were ontological differences between Eastern and Western mentalities (Said 1985:259). Jeremias writes: "It is not the purpose of either parable [the mustard seed and the leaven] merely to describe a process — that would be the way of the Western mind. The oriental mind includes both beginning and end in its purview, seizing the paradoxical element in both cases" (1963:148). Such comparisons reinforce essentialism and become the template for racial determinism and the inferiorizing of the Other, in contrast to Western rationality and superiority. Those who have been part of the colonial experience are well aware that stereotyping is one of the mechanisms by which the colonializer distorts and dominates the Other. Jeremias's comments resemble those of the colonial administrators and missionaries who sought to define the Other by contrasting the superiority of Western civilization to noble savages and inferior races. As Said has pointed out, "[T]he Orient has helped to define Europe (or the West) as its contrasting image, idea, personality, experience" (1985:1–2).

One of the embedded ideas of Orientalism is its perpetuation of the view that Orientals are prone to emotionalism and incapable of rational analysis. Translated into biblical scholarship, this means that Western exegetical efforts are a cerebral and intellectual activity, whereas ours are vague and practical. They investigate and interrogate the texts, and engage in critical analysis; we deal with people and their pressing social, theological, and spiritual concerns. They get to think, while we, meanwhile, feel for the weak and the vulnerable. I would like to use the recent volume that I edited, *Voices from the Margin: Interpreting the Bible in the Third World* (1991), as an example of this perception. When reviewing the book, even a person like Christopher Rowland, who is sympathetic to our cause, comments that "the strength of the Third World exegesis does not lie in its ability to revitalize the historical-critical method by supplying information hitherto unavailable. Rather, the insights it has to offer arise from the articulation of a way of reading in which the perspective of the marginal sheds fresh light on the texts and how they may contribute to our understanding of discipleship" (1992: 45–46). One comment in the "Books Received" section of the *Journal of Biblical Literature* (vol. 110 [1991]: 759) is equally interesting: "This volume contains 34 essays, including an introduction and postscript by the editor, by 28 Latin American, Asian, Native-American, African and African-American contributors, but only those essays in 'Part II — Re-use of the Bible: Examples of Hermeneutical Explorations,' are of biblical interest." The implication seems to be that all historical, exegetical, and intellectual activities are assigned to Western scholars, and we are asked to articulate from the realm of emotion and experience.

Such attitudes, however sincere they may be, reinscribe the popular perceptions of third world interpretation, namely, that we are good at drawing theological implications but weak at undertaking original historical investigation. Western biblical scholars extract deep historical truths from the texts, while we provide homiletical guidelines for Christian living. Such a division of labor not only raises questions about the nature and purpose of historical investigation but also rules out the possibility of culturally informed historical research. Two examples — from Malawi and India — come to mind. A. C. Musopole places witchcraft terminology, which is normally dismissed by Western scholars brought up with Enlightenment values as illogical and antisocial, in its socio-medical context, and from this angle investigates Psalm 18:2 and John 6:50–71. His rereading of these two texts provides an example of how cultural nuances can provide critical resources to illuminate the historical setting of the texts (Musopole 1993). Similarly, Daniel L. Smith-Christopher has shown how Mahatma Gandhi's culturally conditioned reading of Daniel 6 as Hebrew *bhakti* and social resistance literature anticipated the current textual-critical questions (1993). The interpretative task then requires that we read from our own social and cultural locations, and interrogate the texts with our different historical questions, to come up with insights about what the texts might have meant historically and what they mean today. The introduction of cultural data, both past and present, will help to expand the historical base of the narratives.

One of the notions Orientalism reinforced is the image of the Eastern Other inhabiting a world seen as eternal and timeless. The Oriental world is represented as static, and incapable of any change. Biblical scholars often unconsciously replicate this notion that the non-Western nations lack vitality and creativity, living in conditions, categories, and with customs that have barely changed since biblical times.

> Those like myself who attempt to teach biblical texts from the so-
> cial science perspective often find that once the ancient Mediterranean
> world view has been established, and the text explicated in the light
> of it, Western students find themselves farther from rather than closer
> to the text, and are left with the question, "so what?" On the contrary,
> those who attempt the same approach in a non-Western context, find
> that the text comes alive to students in a way that it was not before.
> This is because they are hearing the text unfolded in their own social
> categories, according to their own world view, instead of through the
> filter of the Western post-Enlightenment paradigm with which they do
> not identify. (Osiek 1992:94)

There are two presuppositions behind these sincere words. First, non-
Western societies are the same as they always have been. The core
cultural values such as honor/shame and pollution/purity of which
Osiek speaks are static, regardless of the lapse of time. The possibility of development and change are denied. Such an attitude also
neutralizes the differences between and within our cultures and amal-
gamates our particular histories into one, concocting a unitary subject.
The other presupposition is the assumption that diverse cultural and religious traditions can be bifurcated into two neat divisions — Western
and non-Western.

Natives Going Oriental

Orientalism is not something confined to Western biblical critics.
Traces are evident in the writings of third world biblical scholars as
well. For example, some third world biblical interpreters appropriate
and assimilate various Orientalistic notions. One among them is the
view that societies are static and remain exactly the same for ages.
Some of these scholars posit that there are reasonable similarities
between the conflict-ridden Palestine of Jesus' time and the present-
day Latin America or Asia. Conditions such as poverty, oppression,
and religious authoritarianism, prevalent in the Roman-occupied setting of Jesus' ministry, are seen as resembling those of the current
South American situation. The following two statements, the first by
Leonardo Boff and the other by Jon Sobrino, replicate the internal
Orientalism of third world scholars:

> The socio-political situation in Jesus' day presents striking parallels to
> the situation that gave rise to Liberation theology in Latin America.
> (Boff 1980:103)

[T]here is a clearly noticeable resemblance between the situation here in Latin America and that in which Jesus lived. (Sobrino 1978:13)

Likewise, the Japanese theologian Hisako Kinukawa sees striking cultural parallels between first-century Palestine and modern-day Japan:

[W]e notice many parallels and similarities between the modern Japanese and ancient Mediterranean cultures. We who share the social scenarios that shaped the perspectives of the people of the early Christian age have an advantage experientially in understanding them. (1994:22)

Such statements take note of formal similarities between first-century Palestine and present-day Latin America or Japan but fail to note the critical differences between the exploitation of first-century Palestine and the neocolonial exploitation of Latin America today, or between ancient Mediterranean cultures and modern Japanese cultures.

Natives Deploying Orientalism for Nationalist Ends

While the West has been using Orientalism to define itself, we also use the constructions of Orientalism to define our identities. The Orientalist projection of a glorious Indian past was seized upon by Indian intellectuals to revive the nationalistic fervor affirming the superiority of Eastern spirituality over decadent Western material values. Even denigrated traits were turned into positive characteristics. Richard Fox's term for this is "affirmative orientalism" (1992:152). The backward rural village is now seen as a self-contained, consensus-led, and debureaucratized community; passivity becomes nonviolence; lack of initiative is seen as a mark of nonpossessiveness, and otherworldliness is turned into spirituality. More important, Indian Christian theologians played a critical role in creating a national consciousness. Viewed by the majority Hindus as antinationals, Christian interpreters delved into the ancient Hindu texts to earn their acceptability as true nationals. These Christians followed the path set by the Orientalists, and saw the recovery of the Indian sacred texts — the *Vedas,* the *Upanishads,* the Dharmsastras, and the *Bhagavad Gita* — the use of the indigenous literary theories such as *dhvani,* and the employment of various philosophical and logical systems as a way of entering into mainstream national life. Comparative studies such as those of the *Gita*

and the Fourth Gospel (Amaladoss 1975) and *Manusmrti* and the Pen-
tateuch (Manickam 1977), and the deployment of the *dhvani* method
(Vandana 1989), are all seen not only as celebrating India's glorious
past, but also as recovering an authentic Indian identity for Christians.
Such hermeneutical endeavors have enabled Indian Christians to get
rid of their antipatriotic label, but also have enabled them to invent
a self-image. Such constructions of nationalism were not only a by-
product of the internalization of an Orientalistic notion of nationalism,
but were worked out within the framework of the Indian classical Sanskritic tradition, and at the expense of neglecting India's vernacular,
oral, and folk categories.

Another aspect of internal Orientalism is the privileging of foreign
languages and foreign texts. For instance, those who write in English
are accorded a privileged status over those who use vernacular languages. One of the achievements of colonial education was to produce
a false consciousness among the colonialized that knowledge in any
field of learning — whether in science, theology, or technology —
could be acquired only through the mediation of modern Western
texts. The internalization of this belief has led to the neglect of modern
sources outside European tradition and scholarship. Some Asian scholars hardly cite works from our own regions. Even when writing about
pain and suffering we rush to Moltmann's *The Crucified God,* almost
forgetting Kitamori (1966). I am not arguing against foreign influence
or borrowing but against our failure to recognize our own worth.

Acquiring New Identities

The idea of nationalism itself currently is going through a severe
reappraisal. Two categories of uprooted people seem to emerge in our
time: voluntary exiles and internal exiles. The former are delocalized
transnationals (cf. Appadurai's term, "Postnational" [1993: 417]) who
are part of the diasporic culture which moves across borders and feels
at home everywhere and nowhere; the latter are the derooted nationals
who find themselves refugees in their own countries, or who move to
another country and live in refugee camps and resettlement reserves.
What unites these two groups is that they both long for a home. The
reality of homelessness is increasingly becoming a new framework
for hermeneutics, and it evokes contrary responses. On the one hand,
global theorists propound a borderless transnationalism which scales
boundaries of nations, territories, and states, while minority communities are engaged in ethnonationalist struggles invoking various kinds

of age-old tribal and indigenous sentiments. Makarand Paranjape calls this subnationalism (1994:76).

In the face of the increasing assault on identity, the challenge for someone like myself is to create a contemporary identity which is eclectic, flexible, peaceful, and (in my case) Sri Lankan. However, Sri Lanka itself has become a highly contested site. In overlapping and multiple axes of identification, two negotiating options are generally held to be open to us: either to say that there is no such thing as Sri Lankanness because it is nonexistent or unclarifiable, or to go to the other extreme and fashion a very narrow and one-dimensional notion of ourselves in territorial and linguistic terms, as various ethnic groups are trying to do. I think there is a third alternative: to position ourselves between and betwixt cultures and countries and engage in a processual hermeneutic. JanMohamed calls this limbo state the "interstitial cultural space" (1992:97). It is a vantage point from which those who are caught amidst several cultures and groups and are unable or unwilling to feel "at home" can come up with unlimited alternative forms of group identity and social arrangement. This is not only a mediating position among communities, cultures, and nations, but also enables us to subject cultures "to analytic scrutiny rather than combining them" (JanMohamed 1992:97).

It is in this uncolonialized space, if there ever is one, that contemporary hermeneutical praxis must reserve for itself the freedom to mix and harmonize, to change and retain various ingredients. Locking oneself into one position will deny oneself available options. This is precisely what Iqbal Ahmed Chaudhary, the narrator in Adib Khan's novel *Seasonal Adjustments* (1994), did not want to happen to his daughter, Nadine. *Seasonal Adjustments* is a novel about moving between Bangladesh and Australia and also coming to terms with mixed marriage — Catholic and Muslim. Keith, the Australian father-in-law, a Catholic, is keen that his granddaughter Nadine be baptized to preserve the family tradition. But the child's father, Chaudhary, is not particularly happy with Keith's brand of Christianity. He feels that the narrowness of a single tradition may handicap his daughter, who is growing up in multicultural Australia. He is more interested that Nadine be exposed to different views and ideas before she works out her own religious stance. In a heated conversation at a family party, Keith, who represents the old single-culture Australia, says in a desperately arrogant voice: "Every child is born into a tradition." Chaudhary replies in an equally irritant tone: "Nadine will be among a slowly growing minority which will learn how to combine traditions. It will not be easy" (1994:85). It is in this "interstitial cultural space" that the postnationals in their metropolis and the subnationals in their refugee settlement will work out a relevant hermeneutics. This, as Chaudhary says, will not be easy.

Works Cited

Amaladoss, M. A. 1975. "An Indian Reads St. John's Gospel." In *India's Search for Reality and the Relevance of the Gospel of John.* Ed. Christopher Duraisingh and Cecil Hargreaves. Delhi: ISPCK, pp. 7–24.

Appadurai, Arjun. 1993. "Patriotism and Its Futures." *Public Culture* 5, 3:411–29.

Boff, Leonardo. 1980. "Christ's Liberation Via Oppression: An Attempt at Theological Construction from the Standpoint of Latin America." In *Frontiers of Theology in Latin America.* Ed. Rosino Gibellini. Maryknoll, N.Y.: Orbis Books; London: SCM Press, pp. 100–134.

Fox, Richard G. 1992. "East of Said." In *Edward Said: A Critical Reader.* Ed. Michael Sprinker. Oxford: Blackwell, pp. 144–56.

Gibson, Margaret D. 1902/3. "On the Parable of the Unjust Steward." *The Expository Times* 14:334.

JanMohamed, Abdul R. 1992. "Worldliness-without-World, Homelessness-as-Home: Toward a Definition of a Specular Border Intellectual." In *Edward Said: A Critical Reader.* Ed. Michael Sprinker. Oxford: Blackwell, pp. 96–120.

Jeremias, Joachim. 1963. *The Parables of Jesus.* Rev. ed. London: SCM Press.

———. 1969. *Jerusalem in the Time of Jesus.* London: SCM Press.

Joseph, George Gheverghese. 1991. *The Crest of the Peacock: Non-European Roots of Mathematics.* Harmondsworth: Penguin Books.

Khan, Adib. 1994. *Seasonal Adjustments.* St. Leonards, England: Allen and Unwin.

Kinukawa, Hisako. 1994. *Women and Jesus in Mark: A Japanese Feminist Perspective.* Maryknoll, N.Y.: Orbis Books; London: SPCK.

Kitamori, Kazoh. 1966. *Theology of the Pain of God.* London: SCM Press. Japanese edition, 1946.

Manickam, T. M. 1977. *Dharma according to Manu and Moses.* Bangalore: Dharmaram Publications.

Musopole, A. C. 1993. "Witchcraft Terminology, the Bible, and African Christian Theology: An Exercise in Hermeneutics." *Journal of Religion in Africa* 23, 4:347–54.

Osiek, Carolyn. 1992. "The Social Sciences and the Second Testament: Problems and Challenges." *Biblical Theology Bulletin* 22, 2:88–95.

Paranjape, Makarand. 1994. "Indian (English) Criticism." *Indian Literature* 160:70–78.

Rowland, Christopher. 1992. Review of *Voices from the Margin,* edited by R. S. Sugirtharajah. *Theology* 95:45–46.

Said, Edward. [1978] 1985. *Orientalism.* Harmondsworth: Penguin Books.

————. 1993. *Culture and Imperialism.* London: Chatto and Windus.

Smith-Christopher, Daniel L. 1993. "Gandhi on Daniel: Some Thoughts on a 'Cultural Exegesis of the Bible.' " *Biblical Interpretation: A Journal of Contemporary Approaches* 1, 3:321–28.

Sobrino, Jon. 1978. *Christology at the Crossroads: A Latin American Approach.* Maryknoll, N.Y.: Orbis Books; London: SCM Press.

Sugirtharajah, R. S., ed. 1991. *Voices from the Margin: Interpreting the Bible in the Third World.* Maryknoll, N.Y.: Orbis Books; London: SPCK.

Vandana, Sister. 1989. *Waters of Fire.* Bangalore: Asia Trading Corporation.

6

Jesus in Saffron Robes?

The "Other" Jesus Whom
Recent Biographers Forget

These books say your Jesus was here.
— The Lama from Hemis Monastery

In this chapter I address the way in which competing and contesting images of Jesus have been constructed by recent Jesus researchers. In doing so, my concern is to point out how these constructions unwittingly fall foul of Orientalism — a critical category refined by Edward Said, which signifies the confluence between knowledge and domination. Orientalism is essentially a way of defining, mapping, and containing the "Other," while holding on to Western power and identity (Said 1985). My concern is also to point out that in making the Near Eastern religious terrain a privileged site for such reconstruals, the current questers have overlooked any possible impact Asian religions might have had on the Jesus movement. Lastly, I am also concerned to place this Jesus debate within the multicultural context of Asia.

Recently there has been a vibrant literary output on the life of Jesus.[1] After a lull and hesitancy among biblical scholars, the current curiosity about the historical Jesus is boosted by the increased access to extracanonical material, new archaeological discoveries, and the use of new methods from unlikely disciplines such as anthropology

---

1. For a helpful summary of these lives of Jesus see Marcus J. Borg, *Jesus in Contemporary Scholarship* (Valley Forge, Pa.: Trinity Press International, 1994), 3–43. For the origins and different stages of this quest, and what is different about it, see Bernard Brandon Scott, "From Reimarus to Crossan: Stages in a Quest," *Currents in Research: Biblical Studies* 2 (1994): 253–80.

and the social sciences. After a long period of projecting a decontextualized and rarified Christ, these recent construals have projected a radically theocentric and a human Jesus directly rooted in his own context. Some place Jesus in his Jewish religious milieu and see him as a charismatic holy man and healer (Geza Vermes) or as an eschatological autonomous prophet (E. P. Sanders), while others place him in his Mediterranean social context and cast him as a Jewish peasant Cynic (John Dominic Crossan), a prophetic rebel (Richard Horsley), or a subversive wisdom teacher (Marcus Borg). This recent foregrounding of Judaism as a dominant hermeneutical key to understanding Jesus and his activities is due partly to the involvement of Jewish scholars in the debate and partly to a slow awakening among Christian scholars to the long-standing anti-Judaic biases in Christian interpretation, which among other things led to the Holocaust. Others situate Jesus in the Hellenistic environment of his time, and see him as a wandering Cynic preacher (Burton Mack, G. Downing).

These portrayals have gone a long way to rectify the images of an abstract, ahistorical, and imperialistic Christ which long dominated Christian thinking. As a result of such portrayals, Jesus becomes more accessible and functions more effectively as an avenue to understanding God. So far this is fine, but this renewed interest has also effectively silenced and erased any possible influence of Eastern religious thought on the lifestyle and thinking of Jesus. The whole enterprise serves as an example of how the dominant discourse holds on to its deep-rooted Eurocentric bias, namely the assertion that anything theologically worthwhile can only emanate from Greco-Judeo traditions. Edward Said's observation about Orientalists applies equally to biblical scholars: "European scholars would continue to see the Near Orient through the perspective of its Biblical 'origins,' that is, as a place of unshakably influential religious primacy" (1985:260). Eurocentrism works on a double premise. It looks to Greece for its intellectual and philosophical roots, and dips into its Judaic heritage for its religious origins.

Hermeneutical Forgetting

The current biographers of Jesus exhibit Orientalist tendencies in the selection and interpretation of data. They ignore the possible presence, impact, and contributions of Eastern thinking in the Mediterranean region during the time in which Christian faith emerged. The post-Alexandrian and post-Buddhist missionary context helped to provide the backdrop for the nascent Christian faith. Alexander went up to the Punjab in the fourth century B.C.E., and the Emperor Asoka sent out his Buddhist missionaries a century later. This being the case, one cannot ignore that the early Christian movement must have been breathing an air made rich by the religions of the East. The Christian faith grew up in a cultural and literary milieu influenced by Indian, Buddhist, and Hindu thought patterns. The trade links between India and the Mediterranean Roman Empire were much busier than has often been credited (Sewell 1904; Rawlinson 1975). Along with merchandise, religious ideas also traveled both to and from the Mediterranean world. Vaishnavism was fairly well organized within the Hindu tradition and known to the Greeks prior to the Christian centuries. Heliodoros, the ambassador to Antiakildas, the King of Taxila, was a convert to Vaishnavism (Arabina Basu 1988:185), while early Christian writers refer to the presence in the area of a group of naked yogis of brahmanical tradition. The edicts of the Emperor Asoka inform us of the presence of Buddhist missionaries in west Asia (thirteenth edict, c. 256 B.C.E.). Theravada Buddhist monks had long been active in Alexandria before the birth of Christianity. The earliest Christian reference to Buddhism is found in the writings of Clement of Alexandria (c. 202), who speaks appreciatively not only of Buddhist philosophy but also of the presence of Buddhist *sramanas* (wanderers). The last of the early Christian writers to make any reference to Buddhism was Jerome (382–420), who in his *Contra Jovianus* refers to Buddha's virgin birth. After the decline of the Roman Empire, the emergence of Islam effectively severed the links between India and the Mediterranean, and, with the descent of the West into the Dark Ages, Buddhism dropped out of Western reflection, and Clement's and Jerome's references were not followed up (Scott 1985:90).

The Indian presence in the Mediterranean world, especially during the formative years of Christianity, and the possible percolation — especially of Buddhist ideas — into Christian thinking were widely acknowledged by earlier Indologists and some of the members of the history of religion school (Garbe 1959). The turn of the century saw the publication of parallels between Buddhist Scriptures and the New Testament narratives, identifying and highlighting close textual resemblances (Edmunds 1908, 1909). This interest slackened somewhat after the First World War. One of the reasons for this slackening was the pressure exerted by the Vatican. Henri de Lubac was one of those silenced and reprimanded by the Vatican, à la Boff, for his open attitude toward the Buddhist Scriptures (Thundy 1993:7).

The present biographers of Jesus are a trifle shy when it comes to examining the influence of Eastern religious traditions on the teaching and lifestyle of Jesus. The Gospel narratives situate Jesus and his activities largely in a rural village context. It would be an error to pretend that the early Christian movement operated in cultural, economic, and social isolation. These scholars, as in the case of those who belonged to the history of religion school, look at the data from the now defunct Near Eastern and Mediterranean religious point of view and not from the perspective of the Asian religions, still among the living religions of the world. They act as if the Mediterranean world were a culturally quarantined zone that had not been infiltrated by Eastern religious thinking. Such a view reinforces the long-held missionary perception that Eastern religious traditions are superstitious, vain, and have nothing significant to contribute to theological development.

The self-censorship (Thundy calls it "critical myopia" [1993:10]) exercised by the present biographers does not permit an acquaintance with other religious resources. They do not give serious consideration to the possibility of the Eastern ascetic tradition having influenced the lifestyle of Jesus at all. The role model for his teaching activities could well have come from the Eastern wandering-saint tradition. The Hebrew prophets, with whom Jesus is often identified, were people of fixed abode and were inspired to proclaim God's message at royal courts or to the monarchs of the nations. Jesus, on the other hand, was like a wandering sadhu going from village to village, accepting food from ordinary people, and dispensing counsel and bringing healing. Present biographers have also failed to note the fascinating similarities between Jesus and Siddhartha.[2] Both wander from their home, spend time in solitude, triumph over temptation, and gather around them disciples or bhikus who, after the death of the two masters, spread the gospel or the *dhamma*. The exception here is Marcus Borg, who does make allusions to the lifestyles of these two religious figures, but shies away from discussing possible mutual influence (Borg 1987:143; 1994:36, 70). These scholars are reluctant to address the claim often made by Hindu scholars that concepts such as loving one's enemies, turning the other cheek, and doing good to those who do harm, which form part of Jesus' message, could well have been due to the influence of Buddhist teaching (Radhakrishnan [1939] 1991:184).

---

2. See Lily de Silva, "Wisdom and Compassion of the Buddha and Jesus Christ in Their Role as Religious Teachers," *Dialogue* 17, 1–3 (1990): 1–28.

Two Traditions as Intertextual Continuum

Building on the earlier comparative works, three recent studies, which the current questers seem not to be aware of, have once again demonstrated textual and conceptual affinities between Buddhist writings and Gospel passages. Interestingly, two of these studies were undertaken not by professional biblical experts but by a historian of religions and an English literary critic. R. C. Amore argues that the "Q" source or the "Sayings Gospel" used by the first three Gospel writers could well have been a Buddhist text (Amore 1978). He reckons that Jesus, drawing both from Jewish and Buddhist traditions, could well have refashioned them to suit the contextual needs of his time. Zacharias P. Thundy, a literary critic, once more calls the attention of scholars to the Indian presence in and Eastern religious influence on the Mediterranean world (Thundy 1993). In pointing out the intertextual nature of some of the sacred writings of both Christians and Buddhists, he concludes that there is a "concealed presence" of Indian ideas and motifs in the Gospel tradition. He questions the often-held Eurocentric view that Buddhism borrowed Christian concepts, establishing that Buddhists had scriptural literature and an agreed canon in the third century before the common era. Moving away from Jesus and focusing on the writings of John, Edgar Bruns has shown that Johannine thought was structurally closer to that of Madhyamika Buddhism than to either Judaic or Hellenistic categories (Bruns 1971).

Establishing correct connections between Buddhist and biblical texts may not be easy. The question that needs to be asked again is to what extent the Gospel writers were influenced directly by Indian religious and philosophical systems, or indirectly through their utilization of gnostic materials, which in turn drew inspiration from Indian religious concepts. The reluctance of the present Jesus biographers to give any weight to such influence does not mean that such claims are not tenable. Their reluctance may be due to the nature of historical tools they use and the presuppositions with which they undertake their investigations. Recently these methods have come under heavy attack, most severely from feminist biblical critics, who have exposed their androcentric biases and partisan nature. Asian biblical scholars may likewise find these biographers' investigations biased against Eastern religions. Rarely does one come across a biblical scholar who is conversant with Hindu and Buddhist texts. As a consequence, there is hardly any dialogue going on between biblical scholars and Indologists.

The other problem for biblical scholars is that they are trained to look for and concerned to establish the unique and the particular. Christian interpreters tend to adopt a slightly derisive attitude toward anything that is not evidently of biblical image or origin. They tend to use the position of others as a foil for Christian self-understanding, thus devaluing the claims of other religions. Such a presupposition provides a wrong starting point for engaging in a comparative study of the cultural transmission of texts.

Locating Hermeneutical Markers
for Asia's Multifaith Context

In conclusion, I should like to situate the quest for the historical Jesus within the context of Asia's religious plurality, and to provide certain pointers. Situating Jesus in this triple context — Jewish, Hellenistic, and Eastern religious — is not to minimize his message. Such positioning will help us extend our horizons and puncture the parochialism that lies behind many Christian assumptions. It will also underline that no religion develops on its own, but grows in interaction with others, fashioning at least some of its own distinctiveness by new combinations of existing elements. John Hull aptly reminds us that

> Every religious tradition was born into a world already full of religions, and has evolved in a continual dialogue with one or several other religions. This pattern of co-existence and mutual influences has differed in, let us say, China on the one hand and the Middle East on the other, but it has always been in the context of relationship. (1994:20–21)

Although religious movements seek to establish an exclusive syntax which is uniquely theirs, religious identities are nevertheless inevitably coalitional. It was Swami Vivekananda who said, "I pity the Hindu who does not see the beauty in Christ's character. I pity the christian who does not reverence the Hindu Christ." Such acknowledgment of cross-fertilization will help point to the creative possibilities of universally held elements in the teaching of Jesus. These common elements should provide a starting point to engage in dialogue with people of other faiths, rather than starting from the traditional missionary view that Christians have superior knowledge of the truth. Such comparative analysis, illuminating and enabling as it is, need not stop with simply cataloging similarities and disjunctures. As a next step it should engage in an ideological and cultural critique of both Christian and other religious traditions and expose their virulent sides.

The picture of Jesus that haunts current biblical scholarship is that of a unilateral individual whose spirit is sustained by his exceptional understanding of God. This reflects the individual and self-contained Western male personality type, rather than a picture that would appeal to the Asian concept of personality, which finds its illumination in the context of others and is determined by social needs and the demands of community.[3] We will be helped in understanding his personality when we see it illuminated by his association with the poor, the sick, the women, the marginalized — associations in which he and those with whom he mixed are mutually dependent. To portray him as a detached individual who had the freedom to shape his destiny independently of his family and group needs, is to read Western notions of personality back into Jesus. In spite of the attempts to place Jesus in his Palestinian social world, the image that emerges is that of an isolated and autonomous figure.

It is also fashionable among these construals to project the Jesus movement as a movement designed as a countercommunity, with its own identity and distinction. Such a notion of a countercultural community, although it has its value, may, if it is pushed too far, cause tensions in Asian and African communities. On the one hand, it may provide a sense of liberation from the conventional constraints imposed on people by some aspects of Asian or African culture. On the other hand, such a concept of community has oppressive connotations, for it tacitly encourages Asian Christians to leave their own cultural heritage and join Christian communities whose lifestyle, organizational structure, and worship largely imitate Western patterns. Thus any portrayals of Jesus and his movement which tend to alienate people from their cultural heritage have to be viewed with caution.

Finally, the academic vigor that current biographers show in investigating the historical Jesus recedes when they apply their findings to concerns for the contemporary world. Apart from Marcus Borg (1994), they do not see any need to make hermeneutical connections between their research and the everyday experience of ordinary believers. For instance, E. P. Sanders, in an otherwise remarkable portrayal of Jesus in his own Jewish milieu, refuses to offer any suggestions as to how the Jesus he has mapped out is relevant to Christian faith and prac-

---

3. Individuality is not exclusively a Western trait, but for how Tamils articulate their individuality, see Mattison Mines, *Public Faces, Private Voices: Community and Individuality in South India* (Berkeley: University of California Press, 1994). He describes the Tamil notion of individuality as the "contextualized individual," meaning that the individuality of people is "recognized within the context of groups where they are known and within which they have a known set of statuses and roles" (21).

tice. He reckons this is a theological problem into which he is "not bold enough to venture" (1985:333–34). Similarly, Crossan declares: "I am, of course, absolutely aware of the theological implications of the historical Jesus but I do not think they are driving the process as far as I am concerned" (1994:152). The artificial dichotomy imposed by Western academics between historical exegesis and theology, between historical facts and faith formulations, does not make sense and represents a fundamental contradiction to an Asian way of thinking. It also raises the question of the accountability and responsibility of the interpreter. The crucial hermeneutical question for Asians is not what the historical Jesus looked like but what he means for today — what significance, perhaps still absolute (theological) significance he retains, not least as a result of being still in some way incarnate in living communities.

In a multireligious context like ours, the real contest is not between Jesus and other savior figures like Buddha or Krishna, or religious leaders like Mohammed, as advocates of the "Decade of Evangelism" want us to believe, it is between mammon and Satan on the one side, and Jesus, Buddha, Krishna, and Mohammed on the other. Mammon stands for personal greed, avariciousness, accumulation, and selfishness, and Satan stands for structural and institutional violence. The question then is whether these religious figures offer us any clue to challenge these forces, or simply help to perpetuate them, and how the continuities rather than contrasts among these savior figures may be experienced and expressed.

Works Cited

Amore, R. C. 1978. *Two Masters, One Message: The Lives and Teaching of Gautama and Jesus.* Nashville: Abingdon.

Arabina Basu. 1988. "Sri Aurobindo on Christ and Christianity." In *Neo-Hindu Views of Christianity.* Ed. Arvind Sharma. Leiden: E. J. Brill, pp. 182–212.

Borg, Marcus. 1987. *Jesus, a New Vision: Spirit, Culture, and the Life of Discipleship.* San Francisco: Harper & Row.

———. 1994. *Meeting Jesus for the First Time: The Historical Jesus and the Heart of the Contemporary Faith.* San Francisco: Harper.

Bruns, Edgar J. 1971. *The Christian Buddhism of St. John: New Insights into the Fourth Gospel.* New York: Paulist Press.

Crossan, John Dominic. 1994. "Responses and Reflections." In *Jesus and Faith: A Conversation on the Work of John Dominic Crossan.* Ed. Jeffrey Carlson and Robert A. Ludwig. Maryknoll, N.Y.: Orbis Books, pp. 142–64.

Edmunds, Albert J. 1908, 1909. *Buddhist and Christian Gospels: Now First Compared from the Originals. Being Gospel Parallels from Pali Texts.* Ed. M. Anesaki. Reprinted with additions. Philadelphia: Innes and Sons.

Garbe, Richard. [1914] 1959. *India and Christendom: The Historical Connections between Their Religions.* LaSalle, Ill.: Open Court.

Hull, John. 1994. "Religionism and Religious Education." Paper delivered at the International Conference on Religion and Conflict, May 1994, Armagh, Northern Ireland.

Radhakrishnan, Sarvepalli. [1939] 1991. *Eastern Religions and Western Thought.* Oxford: Oxford University Press.

Rawlinson, H. G. 1975. "Early Contacts between India and Europe." In *A Cultural History of India.* Ed. A. L. Basham. Bombay: Oxford University Press, pp. 425–41.

Said, Edward W. [1978] 1985. *Orientalism.* Harmondsworth: Penguin Books.

Sanders, E. P. 1985. *Jesus and Judaism.* London: SCM Press.

Scott, David. 1985. "Christian Responses to Buddhism in Pre-medieval Times." *Numen* 32, 1:88–100.

Sewell, R. 1904. "Roman Coins Found in India." *Journal of Royal Asiatic Society* 36:591–637.

Thundy, Zacharias P. 1993. *Buddha and Christ: Nativity Stories and Indian Traditions.* Leiden: E. J. Brill.

POSTSCRIPT

7

Cultures, Texts, Margins

A Hermeneutical Odyssey

I would like to begin by sharing with you two texts, both from colonial narratives. The first is from the Church Missionary Society *Register* of 1818 and concerns a conversation between a group of Indians who had gathered around a tree outside Delhi, and a Christian catechist named Anund Messeh. Seeing that these people had Gospel portions with them, Anund tells one of the elderly men, "These books teach the religion of the European Sahibs. It is THEIR book; and they printed it in our language, for our use." In the ensuing conversation, the elderly man replies, "That is true; but how can it be the European Book, when we believe that it is God's gift to us? He sent it to us at Hurdwar. God gave it long ago to the Sahibs, and THEY sent it to us" (Fisher 1818:18).

The second comes from a children's novel, *The History of Little Henry and His Bearer,* by Martha Mary Sherwood, who engaged in evangelical-educational work in India during the colonial days. Sherwood's work epitomizes the vast quantity of children's literature produced before the 1857 Sepoy Mutiny that was influential in forming colonial attitudes and shaping colonial narratives. *The History of Little Henry and His Bearer* is a moral tale about a Scripture-quoting Anglo-Indian, Henry L., aged seven or eight, and his attempts to convert his Indian bearer called Boosy. In one scene of Henry and Boosy traveling to Calcutta, little Henry observes:

> Boosy, this is a good country: that is, it would be a very good country, if the people were Christians. Then they would not be so idle as they now are: and they would agree together and clear the jungles, and build churches to worship God in. It will be pleasant to see people, when

they are Christians, all going on a Sunday morning to some fair church built among those hills, and to see them in an evening sitting at the door of their houses reading the *shaster* — I do not mean your *shaster*, but our *shaster,* God's book. (1821:76–77)

I recount these two narratives to reiterate the point that, although the Bible originated largely in west Asia, when it was received in and introduced to the rest of the continent it was seen as an alien text. Thus an Asian Christian reading of the Bible has never been an easy, natural reading. It is not a spontaneous reading as is a Hindu reading of the *Gita* or a Buddhist reading of the *Dhammapada*. It has always been a confected, mapped, or manufactured reading worked out amidst different cultures and multiple texts and undertaken inevitably from a situation of marginality. Over the years, this artificial reading has produced a variety of readers — readers with certain pre-understandings. Based on the categories of readers described by C. D. Narasimhaiah, the Indian English professor, I identify five types.

1. The *Achariya:* the discriminating reader, the one who puts into practice what is read.

2. The *Panditha:* the academic reader, the one who has considerable knowledge, but is not necessarily a committed reader.

3. The *Bhakta:* the devoted reader, the reader with a cause and commitment.

4. The *Rasika:* the aesthetic reader, the reader who reads for satisfaction and whose interest ceases the moment expectations are satisfied.

5. The *Alpabuddhijana:* the ignorant reader, a reader with an inferior taste. (1994:8, 9)

Of course these reading positions are not hierarchical, nor are there clear-cut divisions. A reader is likely to identify with a combination of these positions. What is crucial for us is that reading involves taking a conscious position.

I would like to narrate briefly the positions we have taken, our hermeneutical journey as Asian readers, the theories we employ to understand our cultures, our texts, our marginality, and also how as interpreters our role has evolved over the years — from being nationalistic to being "postnational." I would like to make it clear that though I use the plural "we," I don't pretend to speak for all Asian interpreters. The concerns I am going to share with you are mine — though some Asian biblical scholars may wish to identify with them.

Colonial Tools and Hermeneutical Wars

As readers we first cut our hermeneutical teeth with colonial methods. When I first started as a theological student, the methods bequeathed to us by Western teachers consisted of various forms of historical criticism. At that time redaction criticism was seen as a major breakthrough. Later, over the years, other approaches such as social science, poststructuralism, narrative theories, and deconstruction were added to the repertoire. Why do I label these supposedly inoffensive and innocent methods colonial? They are colonial not only in origination, style, content, execution, and ideology, but also in the sense that they were used to reshape our minds. Cultural critics have recently been telling us that the lasting effect of imperialism was not only its political subjugation of people or the economic or ecological devastation it caused, but the ideological and cultural vision it implanted among its subjugated people. The famous minute that T. B. Macaulay wrote in 1835 on how to educate Indians is a testimony to colonialist intentions to control culturally the minds of Indians:

> We must at present do our best to form a class who may be interpreters between us and the millions whom we govern; a class of persons, Indian in blood and color, but English in taste, in opinions, in morals and in intellect. (Young 1935:359)

In other words, much more than territorial and political domination, it was the intellectual and cultural control of the natives which was effective in sustaining colonialism, and also of course in perpetuating its motifs and forms in the postcolonial context. In *Culture and Imperialism,* Edward Said writes:

> [T]he imperial dominion itself, its influence is only now beginning to be studied on the minutiae of daily life[,]...the imperial motif woven into the structures of popular culture, fiction, and the rhetoric of history, philosophy, and geography....I am discussing an ideological vision implemented and sustained not only by direct domination and physical force but much more effectively over a long time by *persuasive means....* At the most visible level there was the physical transformation of the imperial realm[,]...the reshaping of the physical environment, administrative, architectural, and institutional feats such as the building of colonial cities....These works show the daily imposition of power in the dynamics of everyday life....But the important factor in these micro-physics of imperialism is that...a unified discourse...develops that is based on a distinction between the west-

erner and the native so integral and adaptable as to make changes impossible. (1993:131–32; italics in the original)

Colonialism is not simply a system of economic and military control, but a systematic cultural penetration and domination. Most damaging is not the historical, political, and economic domination, but the psychological, intellectual, and cultural colonization. Hence, historical-critical methods were not only colonial in the sense that they displaced the norms and practices of our indigenous reading methods, but in that they were used to justify the superiority of Christian texts and to undermine the sacred writings of others, thus creating a division between us and our neighbors. Such materials function as masks for exploitation and abet an involuntary cultural assimilation.

These methods are colonial because they insist that a right reading is mediated through the proper use of historical-critical tools alone. For example, look at the opening lines of George Strecker's *The Sermon on the Mount: An Exegetical Commentary* (1988): "No proper exegesis of the Sermon on the Mount can ignore the results of more than two hundred years of historical-critical research into the New Testament."[1] The statement at the outset rules out the right of a reader or an interpreter to use any other means to understand the text, and those who do not practice these methods are outside the circle. The implication is that the Western academy sets the ground rules for interpretation and defines what tools shall be used, and these tools are paraded as universally applicable in opening the biblical text. Anyone who does not employ them or does not engage with them is an outcast. The inference is that any culturally informed reading by a Gandhi, a Tilak, or a Krishna Pillai is ruled out. In other words, a culturally diversified approach will never get a look. The West not only provides the tools but it also controls our textual preferences. What the Indian social scientist Ashis Nandy said about colonialism applies equally to biblical interpretation: "The West has not merely produced modern colonialism, it informs most interpretations of colonialism. It colors even the interpretation of interpretation" (1991:xii). Seree Lorgunpai, the Thai biblical scholar, narrates an example of how hermeneutical parameters set to work in the Western context make little sense when applied cross-culturally. He says that Westerners find the book of Ecclesiastes strange, but Thai Christians feel at home with it because

---

1. I owe this point to Daniel Patte. See his "Textual Constraints, Ordinary Readings, and Critical Exegesis: Androcritical Perspective," *Semeia* 62 (1993): 62.

of its resemblance to Buddhist teaching. However, when missionaries started to translate the Bible, Ecclesiastes

> was almost one of the last books to be translated, perhaps because the translators were not aware of the similarity between it and Buddhism or they just chose to ignore the connection between them. (1994:155–56)

Once the rules have been established, those who fail to follow them are seen as outcasts, outside the system. They are not regarded as doing proper exegesis.

The methods are colonial because they would have us believe that they have universal validity and significance, although they emerged as a contextual response to the specific needs of Western academies. Essentially they are symbols and products of Western culture. What is colonial is the assumption and claim Western scholars make that their work is universal, comprehensive, and exhaustive. A tacit assumption exists among Western biblical interpreters that their exegetical works and literary productions on the Bible speak for all and cover the concerns of Asia, Africa, and Latin America. If one goes through some of the recent literature on biblical hermeneutics, the unwritten assumption is that they are dealing with global biblical issues. This applies even when the works are excellent and meticulously researched — such as the work of Duncan S. Ferguson, Robert Morgan, and John Barton; Tom Wright's update of Stephen Neill's *The Interpretation of the New Testament, 1861–1961;* and Steven L. Mackenzie's and Stephen R. Haynes's work on theories of biblical criticism. The questions they address — from demythologization to deconstruction, from historical methods to literary theories — are in essence Western questions faced, not necessarily by ordinary persons in the West, but by a group of Western academics who are trying to come to terms with the Bible as a piece of literature and its capacity to illuminate their situation. These volumes assume that the responsibility for interpreting the Bible lies in the hands of Western interpreters and that their theories have universal validity. These volumes do not include or address any Asian or, for that matter, African or Latin American hermeneutical concerns, or mention the interpreters concerned with them. Incidentally, the only non-Westerner who gets a look in these volumes is Gustavo Gutiérrez. He is included not because of his biblical work but because of his prominent role in the liberation theology movement. Perhaps the authors assume that Asian biblical questions are too theological, and Asians as such should not get involved in producing theories because Western exegetical theories will cover Asian concerns.

The institutionalization of these methods in Asian theological colleges has succeeded in producing successful mimics, imitators, translators, rewriters, and even plagiarists among us. Ironically, we began to compare our own interpreters to those in the West to establish our credibility. We hailed Kosuke Koyama as the Karl Barth of Asia or M. M. Thomas as the Niebuhr of India, but in our blind enthusiasm we never bothered to find out who was the C. S. Song of America or the Aloysius Pieris of England. Our hermeneutical arena was littered with exotic symbols and Western hermeneutical figures who had little time for our aesthetic assumptions. Some of them did not even have the remotest understanding of any of the Asian cultures and, worse, betrayed their Eurocentrism in their exegetical judgments. Though Edward Said's celebrated book *Orientalism* features only the work of one Western biblical scholar, Ernest Renan, one can, in fact, see indications of Orientalism in the work of a number of them.

Unfortunately the example I am going to highlight comes from the writings of Joachim Jeremias, whose work I admire and value. Some of the exegetical judgments Jeremias makes in his near-classic *The Parables of Jesus* betray a Eurocentric perception of the Orient. For instance, Jeremias makes an amazing exegetical comment when the steward in the parable of the wicked servant in Luke 16, on hearing of the imminent arrival of his master, alters the debtors' accounts. He justifies the bizarre behavior of the steward on grounds that people in the East do not know anything about bookkeeping or audits (1963:181). At one stroke, he not only claims special European achievements in accounting, but also denies the possibility that other cultures have different ways of accounting. In other words, he excludes the contributions the Chinese, Indians, and Egyptians have made toward the development of present-day mathematics — a point cogently put forward by George Gheverghese Joseph in his recent book, *The Crest of the Peacock: Non-European Roots of Mathematics* (1991). Jeremias makes negative comments about Eastern people throughout the book. I am not questioning his integrity, but Jeremias has unconsciously perpetuated an image of non-Western cultures as lacking vitality, competence, and creativity. Comments on the same parable, which appeared in the *Expository Times* at the height of the colonial era, are also worth recalling. Commenting on the action of the steward who adjusts the accounts, Margaret D. Gibson, writing from Cambridge, suggested that this was a custom which prevailed "whenever Orientals are left to their own methods, uncontrolled by any protectorate of Europeans" (1902/3:334).

Before anyone gets the impression that all Western reading methods are evil and that we are being crushed under their burden, let me assure you that these methods are alive and kicking in our own theological institutions and used with great enthusiasm, even when they are under scrutiny in the West. Our attitude to historical-critical methods is somewhat similar to our use of the English language that we inherited from the imperialists. We do not see the English language as a sign of imperialism but as a vehicle, in Gayatri Chakravorty Spivak's phrase, for "epistemic transformation," namely for transforming the way in which objects of knowledge, especially about humanity, are articulated. Interestingly, some of us use the very method seen as colonial to amplify a variety of subaltern voices — Indian dalits, Japanese burakus, Korean minjung, indigenous people, and women. These tools have been viewed as an effective weapon of decolonization. For instance, recent exegetical examples of minority discourse worked out by Ahn Byung Mu, Kuribayashi Teruo, Hisako Kinukawa, and James Massey may appear to be original Korean, Indian, or Japanese products, yet in a subtle manner they are based on and rework historical-critical principles. It is worth noting that most of these authors are transplanted or uprooted professionals who return to their caste, community, or tribe to re-present themselves as articulate members of various subaltern groups after learning their craft and Western theories of oppression at cosmopolitan centers. Since they are denied entry into the local mainstream interpretative arena, they adopt a negative attitude to their local traditions and share an antagonistic relationship to the dominant culture; hence they are attracted to these foreign theories. Dalit hermeneutics is a good example. Even a casual reader will notice the tendency to dismiss anything Indian as part of the oppressive brahmanical discourse. Whether caste-based hermeneutics will find its solution in foreign-based theories is something the dalits will have to ask themselves.

From Colonialism to Orientalism

Those who have studied the effects of colonialism will say that a colonialized person goes through two conflicting processes. In the first stage, he or she will imitate the colonizer; in the second stage he or she will try to recover indigenous history and retrieve native characteristics. Like the prodigal son, after riotous living among the academic fleshpots of the West and dabbling in fashionable theories, and having our academic purity defiled, we decided to become natives again. Indian social thinkers egged us on. The National Christian Council of India's consultation on "New Patterns of the Social Witness in India" in 1960 encouraged us to explore our own cultural and philosophical resources. The findings of the consultation state:

> At the present time very few Christians are making any serious study of Indian philosophy, history and social thought. Many of us are not aware of our intellectual heritage.... Since most of us are not adequately informed, we are not able to contribute our share to the thinking in these spheres.[2]

Gora, the eponymous hero in Rabindranath Tagore's novel, echoed our sentiments.

> If we have the mistaken notion that because the English are strong and we can never become strong unless we become exactly like them, then that impossibility will never be achieved, for by mere imitation we shall eventually be neither one thing or the other.... come inside India, accept all her good and her evil: if there be deformity then try and cure it from within but see it with your own eyes, understand it, think over it, turn your face towards it, become one with it. (1989:102)

We learned the same from Frantz Fanon, that it would be better for us to be natives at the uttermost depths of our wretchedness than to be like our former master. In our enthusiasm to assert our nationalism we searched for indigenous methods. As an alternative to the importation of inappropriate theories of interpretation, we turned our attention to distinctive national theories for inspiration and for new directions. We saw this revival of methods of a bygone era as a way of celebrating and elevating our Asian identity.

In the name of indigenization, we were happy to fill our hermeneutical arena with ancient symbols, stories, and rites, ignoring the crude realities of our present which was replete with religious rivalries, caste hierarchies, and social inequalities. Blissfully and unconsciously we were constantly being born and reborn into the past. Among the many things Western Orientalists manufactured for us was a glorious past in the Sanskritic tradition. At this juncture, the ancient theories of Sanskrit poetics came to our rescue. To our delight we discovered that

---

2. See "Nasrapur Findings IV: Christians and Cultural Foundations of New India," *Religion and Society* 7, 1 (1960): 68–72. Quote is from p. 70.

even before the interpretative theories were worked out in the West, classical writers in Sanskrit literature had come up with extremely sophisticated and well-developed theories of reading. We were proud to claim and celebrate Panini as the world's first grammarian, and ecstatic to know that there was a school of exegetes, the Mimamsakas, concerned with determining the correct meaning of texts and settling dubious or problematic passages. It dawned on us that we could profitably employ various theories of meaning worked out by Sanskritic theoreticians. We encountered the theory of *rasa*, propounded by the sage Bharata in the fifth century, which holds that poetry is essentially an emotive discourse. There was Ksehemendra's *auchita*, translated as "propriety," a harmonious adaptation of language, figure, imagery, and so forth. Then there was *dhvani,* expounded by Anandavardhana in the ninth century, which stresses the suggestive possibility of a text, its evocative nature, and its emotional grip on the reader, hearer, or spectator.

We were ecstatic. But our excitement was short-lived. There was no sustained effort to produce exegetical examples illustrating how these methods would work with biblical texts. A feeble attempt in the late 1970s used the *dhvani* method as a way of dispensing with Western methods. A special issue of *Bible Bhashyam,* the Indian biblical quarterly, featured articles with exegetical examples. Sister Vandana and Anand Amaladass came to be closely associated with this method. However, the enthusiasm for this method waned when serious questions were posed about the whole idea of indigenization. Now, on looking back, we realize that our attempts to search for indigenous methods had inadvertently contributed to a new form of Orientalism, but Orientalism in reverse, developed this time by the natives themselves. To use Edward Said's phrase, we were participating in our own Orientalizing (1985:325). We were tacitly acquiescing in and reinforcing the images and theories Western Orientalists created about us. These Orientalists provided us with a new self-perception of ourselves, and it was they who led us to believe in past glories and who made us fantasize about their possible return, in the process causing us to forget present needs and future challenges. Fanon long ago cautioned in effect that any mindless appropriation of customs and rituals divorced from their historical context not only goes against present realities but also hurts the very people it intends to serve. He warned us that "the desire to attach oneself to tradition or bring abandoned tradition to life does not only mean going against the current history but also opposing one's own people" (1990:180). We realized that our efforts to create an India of our dreams, as a reaction to the continual threat of the universalizing nature of Western theories, divorced us from current reality and history, and in a way worked against our own people — namely the dalits, the indigenous people, and women. We were using the very brahmanical discourse which kept these people outside the mainstream. Paradoxically, the use of an indigenous method ended up being condemned as elitist, oppressive, and alienating.

From Orientalism to Nativism

While some were busy trying to recover Sanskritic concepts, others who were not part of or influenced by this movement, but were suffocating under the double burden of Western and Sanskritic theories, were equally busy trying to animate our own *bhasa* or vernacular tradition. Students of Indian culture draw an important distinction between the *Marga,* the high road, and *Desi,* the country road. Sanskrit, which is seen as pan-Indian, ancient, and reputable — and has hallowed texts — is regarded as the *Marga,* while local and vernacular languages of India are seen as the *Desi.* The Indian literary critic G. N. Devy calls the search for models in the vernacular tradition nativism:

> It views literature as an activity taking place "within" a specific language...and bound by the rules of discourse native to the language of its origin. It understands writing as a social act, and expects of it an ethical sense of commitment to the society within which it is born. It rules out the colonial standard of literary history...and the *marga* claim of the mainstream literature as being the only authentic literature. (1992:119–20)

In other words, nativism is a hermeneutical enterprise which takes place within a specific cultural and language matrix, bound by the rules set by that language.

Nativism draws on both performance and textual traditions. The biblical reflections of Sadhu Sundar Singh, Mungamuri Devadas, Vaman Tilak, Paul Kadamabhavanam, and H. A. Krishna Pillai borrow largely from the vernacular mode of storytelling. Hermeneutics, for them, is not only rereading the ancient texts but also retelling old stories for a new context. They articulated their expositions in their own mother tongues — Punjabi, Telugu, Marathi, and Tamil. Most of them were converts from Hindu faith, familiar with the digressive narrative mode, and influenced by their vernacular narrative thinking. Their retellings of the Christian stories are cyclical, episodic, and full of asides and parentheses. There are others who draw from the vernacular secular literary tradition. Recently, Dayanandan Francis, applying the devices of Tamil *aham* poetry — the love poems of Tamil literature — has renarrativized the Song of Songs, with the characterization based on the Sankam tradition of *thalaivan* (lover) and *thalaivi* (beloved) (1992). Adigalar Lawrence, who sees "biblical ideals inherent in the culture of Tamils," likens the concept of redemption in the Bible to the concept mentioned in the ancient Tamil literature called *Tholkapiam.*

> A parallel could be drawn between the Genesis story of Satan entering into the garden of Eden to establish dominion over the creature of God and God redeeming the fallen human beings with the story of *Vetchi and Karanthai thinai.* (1993:72)

He reckons that the study and use of Tamil alone provides the key for indigenizing interpretation (73).

Nativism also draws inspiration from vernacular religious texts, especially from the bhakti — devotional writings. Two interpreters come to mind — H. A. Krishna Pillai and A. J. Appasamy. As a devotee of Lord Visnu, Krishna Pillai found it difficult to understand the juridical image of expiation used by the pietistic German missionaries to explain the work of Christ. He felt such imagery was a hindrance. Instead, he drew on his own Vaisnavite heritage to arrive at an understanding of the work of Christ. He reimaged the cross-event as God releasing precious life to make Krishna Pillai a devotee. The first poetry Krishna Pillai wrote after his conversion has no reference to a juridical transaction.

Appasamy advocated the use of bhakti/devotional poets from both Saivite and Vaisnavite traditions to enrich Christian theology. His books, *Christianity as Bhakti Marga* (1928) and *What Is Moksa?* (1931), are expositions of the mysticism of John's Gospel. The Johannine narratives are illuminated by a wealth of illustrations from bhakti poets such as Manickavachakar, Nammalvar, Tayumanavar, Ramalinga Swami, Tukaram, Kabir, and Guru Nanak. By establishing interconnections between these and Christian texts, and by coalescing different spiritual traditions, Appasamy contended that these Indian sages belonged to Indian Christians as much as to Hindus, Muslims, and Sikhs. The exegetical insights of Krishna Pillai and Appasamy fall under the rubric of cultural exegesis, in which Daniel Christopher-Smith is currently engaged and trying to promote, but the term "nativism" may also be helpful in some respects.

Vernacular hermeneutics promoted the awareness of various indigenous traditions. It also compensated for the Orientalists' regrettable neglect of literatures in non-Sanskritic traditions. It called into question the hegemonic status of Sanskrit and opened up multiple performance and textual traditions. Significantly, it helped to restore the balance by offering an alternative classical culture in Tamil and paved the way for the shift from vedic vision to bhakti. The problem with the vernacular hermeneutics is its isolationism and protectionism. It is culture-bound and, hence, always in danger of being ghettoized, understood only by the insiders and irrelevant to the majority. It is accorded privileged status because it is uncontaminated by external influences. We need to ask again in an emerging complex of global relations whether we can still talk of a pure culture which is not corrupted by the globalization process.

One of the significant contributions of Orientalist and nativist approaches is that they give back to people their lost memory — a memory erased by Western discourse. When Chamcha, the postcolonial cosmopolitan Indian, in Salman Rushdie's *The Satanic Verses,* lists his favorite movies, predictably all Western masterpieces, another character, Gibreel, exclaims, "You've been brainwashed. All this arthouse crap," and proceeds to give his list of popular Indian cinema. He tells Chamcha: "Your head is full of junk. You have forgot everything worth knowing" (1988:439–40). What was ironic about the whole indigenization process was that while Christians were trying to recover elements from the ancient past, or, as Fanon would have put it, "mummified figments," other Asian religions such as Buddhism and Confucianism were trying to modernize and accommodate themselves to the new urban industrial culture sweeping through Asia (Tamney 1993:65). While we were trying to promote the idea of the distant past as normative, the regional religions of Asia were trying to update and recast their basic tenets to meet the challenges of industrial development.

Let me pause here for a while and share some of the hermeneutical dilemmas we face. There is, of course, the dilemma presented by our tendency to harmonize, which India's ever recurring religious multiplication makes a constant necessity, but which does not always make it easy to take an unwavering position. Another question that comes to mind is — why do we need theories? Like Gita Das, the heroine in Kirin Narayan's novel, I too wonder whether we should analyze "everything in terms of hidden structures, themes, intentions," and in so doing lose the pleasure of a good read (1994:85). I would like to ask with the Indian critic Devy (1992:121) if theorizing is a colonial compulsion? Are we wasting our critical talents in the pursuit of such theories? Is biblical criticism really an important activity in its own right? Is it an escapist activity in which critical theorization replaces original production, and critical work replaces our ethical responsibilities? What is the purpose of our reading practice? Is it to produce subtle nuances of emotion and feeling in individuals, or to help communities to face the problems of the contemporary world, as Käsemann proposed:

> I do not know Dom Helder Camara personally, and he — an out and out conservative in comparison with myself — will be unacquainted with my work. But were my work no possible help to him in his troubles, I will not want to remain a New Testament scholar. No real service is rendered to the Spirit by one who is unable to assist men under trial. (1973:236)

What then is the task of a hermeneut? Is it to change the world or to understand it? Recently Chaturvedi Badrinath argued for an inversion of Marx's eleventh thesis that the philosophers have so far tried to interpret the world, with the point, however, being to change it. Badrinath turns this around — "Reformers have so far tried to change India; the point however is to understand India" (1993:29). Perhaps in the process some service will be rendered, such as Käsemann proposed.

Searching for a Role:
From Nationalism to Postnationality

Little attention has been paid to the social history of the emergence of Asian theological reflection. Unlike modern Christian theology in the West, which emerged amidst various philosophical trends — capitalism, industrial revolution, secularism, and interdenominational squabbles — in India it arose as the result of the English-educated middle-class Christians attempting to imagine a modern nation. The beginnings of Indian Christian interpretation lie in the encounter between the imported colonial denominational theologies and the newly converted Indian Christians trying to assert their Indian identity in the face of the dominant Western culture. Thus it was in response to colonialism, and the need to construct a homogeneous and unifying Indian culture as opposed to the existing multifaceted cultural practices, that early Christian converts in India began to imagine the nation as a unified, pan-Indian entity. The 1857 revolt, which was the beginning of

Indian nationalism, was a turning point also in Indian Christian theological reflection. Several examples of national stirring (K. Baago's phrase) took the form of opposition to the colonial theology. When Indian converts of the nineteenth century found themselves faced with a dual existence — their Indian heritage and their Christian faith — and found that the missionaries of that time would not give them freedom in the exercise of their faith, some of them, under the leadership of Lal Behari, a Calcuttan writer and pastor, declared in their journal, the *Bengal Christian Herald:*

> In having become Christians, we have not ceased to be Hindus. We are Hindu Christians, as thoroughly Hindus as Christians. We have embraced Christianity, but we have not discarded our nationality. We are as intensely national as any of our brethren of the native press can be. (Baago 1968:3)

This national spirit continued even after independence, when Indian theologians saw their task as helping to build the nation after the end of the colonial era. The theological writings of M. M. Thomas, E. V. Mathew, and Paul Devanandan bear witness to their patriotic consciousness and show these theologians beginning their task of recovering the biblical message to build up the nation after the ravages of colonialism. The Sri Lankan, Celestine Fernando, captures the mood:

> We have been convinced by the pressure of events in our country, over-population, undernourishment, unemployment, grossly inadequate housing, racial conflicts, political corruption, ... to show the relevance of the Bible for nation-building today. (1981:185)

But today, after nearly forty years of independence and postcolonial rule, the concept of the nation-state has come under severe scrutiny. India may look like a valid cultural label on a map, but the question of what it means to an Indian or a Sri Lankan is increasingly difficult to answer in the face of rapid globalization and internationalization. Arjun Appadurai, the social scientist, attributes the emergence of this global culture to five linked dimensions of cultural flow moving across national boundaries: ethnoscape, technoscape, finanscape, mediascape, and ideoscape. The suffix "scape" indicates the varying and unfixed nature of these landscapes and their "historical, linguistic, and political situatedness" (1990:7).

1. "Ethnoscape" means the landscape of persons who constitute the shifting world in which we live — tourists, immigrants, refugees, exiles, guest workers, and other moving groups and persons.

2. "Technoscape" means the flow of mechanical and informational technology across "previously impervious boundaries," through multinational corporations.

3. "Finanscape" means the rapid flow of money through currency markets, national stock exchanges and commodity speculation.

4. "Mediascape" means the distribution of the electronic capabilities to produce and disseminate information through such media as newspapers, magazines, TV, and films.

5. "Ideoscape" means the flow of ideas, terms, and images often organized around such key words as freedom, welfare, rights, sovereignty, and, these days, democracy. (1990:6–11)

Thus, according to Appadurai, the constant flow of persons, technologies, finance, information, and ideology results in deterritorialization, which in his view is "one of the central forces of the modern world" (1990:11). Appadurai neither rules out the existence of "relatively stable communities and networks" nor refutes the current tribalism around the world. But he contends that "the warp of these stabilities is everywhere shot through with the woof of human motion, as more persons and groups deal with the realities of having to move or the fantasies of wanting to move" (1990:7). This large-scale movement of people, within and between countries, has created dislocation, homelessness, and disorientation. Homesickness has become the cultural characteristic of our time. One of the stories in Salman Rushdie's recent collection of short stories, *East, West,* raises precisely this issue. "At the Auction of the Ruby Slippers" is a parable about homelessness in which the exiles, displaced persons, political refugees, and orphans perceive that the possession of magic slippers guarantees not only protection against witches, but is a safe promise to journey back home. But the question is, where is home?

The exceptional movement of people has resulted for a variety of reasons in the emergence of the diasporic interpreter, who is likewise constantly in search of home. Those of us who are part of the diaspora are equally committed to and disturbed by both cultures — the one we left behind and the one we enter and try to understand. To use Abdul R. JanMohamed's phrase, "we are specular border intellectuals" endeavoring to stand among and not fall between many stools. JanMohamed defines the "specular border intellectual" as a person caught between several cultures and groups, and who subjects these cultures "to analytic scrutiny rather than combining them," and "utilizes his or her interstitial cultural space as a vantage point from which to define, implicitly or explicitly, other utopian possibilities of group formation" (JanMohamed 1992:97). We have multiple belongings and multiple loyalties, and, as the demoniac in Mark's Gospel said, we are many. The Iraqi journalist Kanan Makiya asks a pertinent question: "What is the connection between the passport one holds, the views one expresses, the books one writes, and one's innermost emotional and belief system, which is of course what constitutes one's identity?" (1994:233).

We have come a long way as interpreters, most of us starting by identifying ourselves with nationalism and patriotic causes. I think we need to reconsider our role as interpreters to take into account the multifaceted and enormously complex web of global and local relations, and to ask ourselves what is the Indianness or Sri Lankanness we are craving. This was what Tagore was trying to address in his novel *Gora,* which I have already mentioned. Written when nationalism was becoming a potent political force against colonialism in India, we see in Gora, the hero of the novel, a passionate defender of all that is Hindu, who sees in his defense a way of overcoming the humiliation of colonialization. But suddenly, to his horror, Gora discovers that he is not only not a Hindu, but not even an Indian. He discovers that he was born to Irish parents. But what Gora learns through the other two characters — Anandamoyi, the surrogate mother who raises him, and Paresh Babu, the Brahmo leader — is that true Indianness transcends India. By their willingness to redefine traditional Indian purity codes, Anandamoyi and Paresh Babu reaffirm a moral universe which Gora finds it difficult to reject. But to Tagore this shared universe is indeed universal, transcending caste, religion, and national boundaries.

At a time when the world is becoming, in Roland Robertson's phrase, "a single place," and the boundaries between cultures are blurring, we have two options as interpreters. Let me illustrate these options with two stories. When Alexander the Great invaded India he wanted to meet the philosophers in Taxila, the ancient university town, which is now part of modern Pakistan. First he sent his representative. The philosophers did not bother to receive him. The king was in a hurry to see them, so he himself made the journey. The guards went ahead of him to announce his coming. On arrival, Alexander spoke about his achievements and announced himself as their new patron. There was no response from the philosophers. The king thought that they had not heard him. So he ventured to move closer. As he moved, the sun came behind him and his shadow fell upon one of the philosophers. The conqueror addressed them again: "I, Alexander the Great, stand before you. All the earth is mine. Speak and tell me what I can do for you. What can I bestow upon you?" The response he got was staggering. The philosopher upon whom the shadow of the conqueror fell replied: "Nothing much. Just move either a little to the right or to the left so that the rays of sun can fall upon me and their heat can warm my body again." The response was a stunning indication that there was no point in fraternization between East and West. The gap looked too wide for reconciliation.

The second story comes from Salman Rushdie's *East, West,* to which I have already referred. The narrator in "The Courter" is an immigrant in England who comes to a different understanding of bicultural marginality and East-West relations. The comma Rushdie places between the words "East" and "West" in the title of the book provides us a clue. At a time when people are concerned with hyphenated identities, Rushdie sees reality from the less polarizing perspective of a comma, with which histories of cultural differences can exist side-by-side in a state of creative interference and interruption.

We either can be, in the words of the Vietnamese writer Le Ly Hayslip, whose life story was immortalized in the movie *Heaven and Earth,* "the people in the middle," or we can identify with the philosophers in Taxila and tell others to move over, thus establishing an irreconcilable chasm. To me it is increasingly becoming clear that cultures, nations, and identities can never be defined in simple binary appositions — East-West, center-margin. If we try to fix everything into neat categories, we may obscure complex perceptions and insights that an ethnocentric approach would permit. In an era of easy polarizations, I for one, like the immigrant narrator in Salman Rushdie's story, would rather live with the complexities than easy binary appositions. I would like to end with the words of the narrator:

> But I, too, have ropes around my neck, I have them to this day, pulling me this way and that, East and West, the nooses tightening, commanding, *choose, choose.* I buck, I snort, I whinny, I kick...I refuse to choose. (1994:211; italics in the original)

Works Cited

Appadurai, Arjun. 1990. "Disjuncture and Difference in the Global Economy." *Public Culture* 2, 2:1–24.

Baago, Kaj. 1968. *Pioneers of Indigenous Christianity.* Madras: Christian Literature Society.

Badrinath, Chaturvedi. 1993. *Dharma, India, and the World Order.* Edinburgh: Saint Andrew Press.

Devy, G. N. 1992. *After Amnesia: Tradition and Change in Indian Literary Criticism.* Hyderabad: Orient Longman.

Fanon, Frantz. [1961] 1990. *The Wretched of the Earth.* Harmondsworth: Penguin Books.

Fernando, Celestine. 1981. "The Use of the Bible in the International Life in Asia." *International Review of Mission* 70, 279:181–88.

Fisher, Rev. Harry. 1818. Letter to Mr. Thomason, 6 May 1817. *Missionary Register* (January).

Francis, Dayanandan T. 1992. *Vuyar Thani Padal.* Madras: Christian Literature Society.

Gibson, M. D. 1902/3. "On the Parable of the Unjust Steward." *The Expository Times* 14:334.

JanMohamed, Abdul R. 1992. "Worldliness-without-World, Homelessness-as-Home: Toward a Definition of the Specular Border Intellectual." In *Edward Said: A Critical Reader.* Ed. Michael Sprinker. Oxford: Blackwell, pp. 96–120.

Jeremias, Joachim. 1963. *The Parables of Jesus.* London: SCM Press.

Joseph, George Gheverghese. 1991. *The Crest of the Peacock: Non-European Roots of Mathematics.* Harmondsworth: Penguin Books.

Käsemann, Ernst. 1973. "The Problem of a New Testament Theology." *New Testament Studies* 19, 3:235–45.

Lawrence, Adigalar T. 1993. "Concept of Redemption and Vetchi and Karanthai." *Arasaradi: Journal of Theology* 6, 1:72–73.

Lorgunpai, Seree. 1994. "The Book of Ecclesiastes and Thai Buddhism." *Asia Journal of Theological Reflection* 8, 1:155–62.

Makiya, Kanan. 1994. *Cruelty and Silence: War, Tyranny, Uprising, and the Arab World.* Harmondsworth: Penguin Books.

Nandy, Ashis. [1988] 1991. *The Intimate Enemy: Loss and Recovery of Self under Colonialism.* Delhi: Oxford University Press.

Narasimhaiah, C. D. 1994. Introduction to *East West Poetics at Work.* Delhi: Sakhitya Akademi.

Narayan, Kirin. 1994. *Love, Stars, and All That.* New Delhi: Penguin Books.

Rushdie, Salman. 1988. *The Satanic Verses.* Harmondsworth: Viking.

———. 1994. *East, West.* London: Jonathan Cape.

Said, Edward. [1978] 1985. *Orientalism.* Harmondsworth: Penguin Books.

———. 1993. *Culture and Imperialism.* London: Chatto & Windus.

Sherwood, Martha Mary. 1821. *The History of Little Henry and His Bearer.* Wellington: F. Houlston and Son.

Tagore, Rabindranath. [1924] 1989. *Gora.* Madras: Macmillan.

Tamney, Joseph B. 1993. "Religion in Capitalistic East Asia." In *A Future for Religion? New Paradigms for Social Analysis.* Ed. William H. Swatos, Jr. London: Sage, pp. 55–72.

Young, G. M. 1935. *Speeches by Lord Macaulay with His Minute on Indian Education.* London: Oxford University Press.

Index

Abhishiktananda, Swami, 6
Abraham, M. V., 11
Achebe, Chinua, 94
Adam, W., 45n.10
Ahn Byung Mu, 129
Aleaz, K. P., 6
Alexander the Great, 114, 138–39
Amaladass, Anand, 6, 131
Amaladoss, M. A., 6
Amore, R. C., 116
Anandavardhana, 6, 131
Andrews, C. F., 55
Anglicism, 8–12, 87–88
anti-Semitism, 81–82
Appadurai, Arjun, 14, 69, 136–37
Appasamy, A. J., 13–14, 133
Arnold, Matthew, 58
Arumainayagam, 81
Asoka, Emperor, 114
auchita method, 131
Aurobindo, 90

Baago, K., 136
Badrinath, Chaturvedi, 135
Banerjea, Krishna Mohan, 4–5
Barker, Ernest, 60n.6, 60–61
Barth, Karl, 10, 128
Barton, John, 127
Behari, Lal, 136
Bhagavad Gita, 63, 73, 90–91, 107–8
Bhagavata Purana, 73
Bhagavatar, Iyadurai, 13
bhakti, 12, 13–14, 133
Bharata, 131
bhasa tradition, 132. *See also* vernacular traditions

Bible Women, 83
biblical theology movement, 10–11
Boff, Leonardo, 106
Borg, Marcus, 113, 115, 118
Boyd, R. H. S., 6
Brahmo Samaj, the, 30, 66
Brown, L. E., 55, 73
Brunner, Emil, 10
Bruns, Edgar, 116
Buchanan, Claudius, 97
Buddhism
    affinities between Gospel passages and texts from, 116
    the book of Ecclesiastes and, 127
    early Christianity and, 114
    Indian Church Commentaries on, 61, 63
    Jesus and, 115
Bultmann, Rudolf, 10–11, 37
burakumin exegesis, 11

"Cambridge Bible for Colleges and Schools," 59
Carey, William, 87–88
caste system, the, 61, 63, 70, 81, 129
Chadwick, Owen, 58
Chao, Phebe Shih, 83
Chow, Rey, ix
Christian Student's Library, 9–10
Christopher-Smith, Daniel, 105, 133
Church Missionary Review, the, 58
citizenship, 68–69
Clement of Alexandria, 114
Cohn, Bernard, 91
Colebrooke, J. H., 4

colonialism
  the Bible and the ideology of, 18–20
  blindness of the Indian Church Commentaries to damage done by, 83–84
  development of Asian theological reflection under, 135–36
  Fanon on, 82, 83
  methods of biblical interpretation and, 125–29
  postcolonialism's critique of, 17–18
  stages scholars go through under the influence of, 129–32
  translation and, 86–92
  See also imperialism
"contact zones," 51
Coomarasawamy, Ananda, 73
Crossan, John Dominic, 113, 119
Crosthwaite, Arthur, 62, 63, 67, 68, 70, 72, 73, 74–75

dalits, 8, 11, 129
de Lubac, Henri, 114
demythologization, 10–11
Devadas, Mungamuri, 13, 132
Devanandan, Paul, 136
Devy, G. N., 132, 135
Dhammapada, 73
Dharmsastras, the, 107
dhvani method, 6, 107, 108, 131
Downing, G., 113
Duff, Alexander, 8

essentialism, 70
Eurocentrism, 16, 82, 103–4, 112–13, 128
exoticism, 69–70

Fanon, Frantz, 8, 18, 82, 83, 130, 131, 134
Farquhar, J. N., 66
feminist theology, 11
Ferguson, Duncan S., 127
Fernando, Celestine, 136
Firminger, Walter Kelly, 65

Foucault, Michel, 42
Fox, Richard, 107
Francis, Dayanandan, 133
Frei, Hans, 37
fulfillment theory, 66

Gandhi, Mahatma, 55, 91, 105, 126
Gates, Henry Louis, 11
George V, King, 4, 68
German scriptural studies, 56, 57
Gibson, Margaret, 104, 128
globalization, 14, 17, 136–37
Gramsci, Antonio, 69
Gregorios, Paul, 6
Gutiérrez, Gustavo, 127

Hall, Stuart, 21
Hanson, Anthony, 10
Haynes, Stephen R., 127
Hayslip, Le Ly, 139
"heathens": use of term, 46–47
hermeneutics
  of authors of Indian Church Commentaries, 54–61
  contrast of liberationist and imperial, 80
  current dilemmas facing Indians regarding, 134–35
  of nativist interpreters, 132–34
  and situating Jesus in an Asian context, 117–19
Hinduism
  Anglicists' view of, 10
  colonialist attitude toward, 87
  early Christianity and, 114
  Hebrew Scriptures and, 81
  Indian Church Commentaries on, 58, 61–63, 64, 66, 73, 74
  Jesus and, 115
  missionaries' view of, 88–89
  and nineteenth-century views of Jesus, 36n.8
  Rammohun Roy/Marshman debate and, 49–50
  reaction by, to concept of fixed, holy text, 90–91

historical criticism, 9, 10, 11, 12, 59, 126, 129
Holmes, W. H. G., 58–59, 61–62
Horsley, Richard, 113
Hort, F. J. A., 55n.3, 56
Huber, Friedrich, 11
Hull, John, 93, 117
hybridity, 16–17

imperialism
 the Bible's context of, 18–20
 biblical hermeneutics and, 54–61
 contradictions in, exposed by biblical commentaries, 79–84
 cultural domination and, 125–26
 exegetical ploys to reinforce, 75–79
 view of colonized established by, 69–75
 See also colonialism
Inden, Roland, 88
Indian Bible Society, 83
Indian Church Commentaries
 Anglicist goals and, 9–10
 background of, 54–55
 blindness to shortcomings of the British Empire, 82–84
 conclusions regarding, 79–84
 hermeneutics of authors of, 55–61
 and methods of colonial power, 69–71
 ploys used to reinforce British colonialism, 75–79
 type of Christianity projected by, 61–69
 view of Indians in, 71–75
Indian Textual Mutiny of 1820
 background of, 29–33
 colonialism's role in, 45–50
 conclusions regarding, 50–52
 discussion of Rammohun Roy's text that incited the, 33–35

 exegetical enactments of Rammohun Roy and Marshman and, 41–45
 Rammohun Roy's hermeneutics and, 35–41
individualism, 118, 118n.3
intertextuality, 93, 116
Islam, 61, 62, 66, 74, 114

JanMohamed, Abdul R., 109, 137–38
Jefferson, Thomas, 34n.7
Jeremias, Joachim, 103–4, 128
Jerome, 114
Jesus
 Eastern influences on, 113–15
 Eurocentrism of studies of the life of, 112–13
 his experience of colonialism, 20
 the Indian Church Commentaries' portrait of, 66–67
 markers for situating, within an Asian context, 117–19
 Rammohun Roy's portrait of, 33–36, 48
 recent works on Buddhism and, 116
 Western view of identity of, 118–19
Jewel in the Crown, The, 84
Jones, William, 4
Joseph, George Gheverghese, 103, 128

Kabir, 73
Kadamabhavanam, Paul, 132
kaletchepam method, the, 13
Kamban, 91–92
Kampchen, Martin, 7
Käsemann, Ernst, 135
Keshub Chunder Sen, 36n.8, 66
Khan, Adib, 109–10
Kinukawa, Hisako, 107, 129
Kipling, Rudyard, 82
Kitamori, Kazoh, 108
Knight, A. M., 55
Koyama, Kosuke, 128

Krishna Pillai, H. A., 13, 14, 126, 132, 133
Ksehemendra, 131
Kuribayashi, Teruo, 129

laksana method, the, 6
Lawrence, Adigalar, 133
Lefroy, G. A., 55
Lessing, G. E., 37
liberation theology, 80, 94
Lightfoot, J. B., 55, 55–56n.3, 56
Ling, Amy, 11
Lorgunpai, Seree, 126–27

Macaulay, T. B., 8–9, 125
Mack, Burton, 113
Mackenzie, Steven L., 127
Makiya, Kanan, 138
Manickam, T. M., 6
Manu, 73
Marshman, Joshua
  debate between Rammohun Roy and, 36–37
  description of Rammohun Roy by, 32
  exegetical principles of, 41, 42, 43–44
  hermeneutics of, 39–41
  implications of his debate with Rammohun Roy, 50–52
  Rammohun Roy's accusations against, 34
  reaction to Rammohun Roy's *Precepts,* 33
  shortcomings of theology of, 45–46
Mary, Corona, 14
Mary, Queen, 68
Massey, James, 129
Mathew, E. V., 136
Matsya Purana, 6
Messeh, Anund, 123
Mimamsakas, 131
minjung, the, 11, 129
missiology, 57

missionaries
  blindness toward Jesus' Asianness, 48
  English biblical hermeneutics and, 54–61
  exegetical principles of, 42
  Hinduism as seen by, 88–89
  Lightfoot on the obstacles for, 55–56n.3
  paternalism of, 71–72
  Rammohun Roy on, 35–41, 44–45, 50
  Western view of Christianity propounded by, 61–69
modernism, 9, 15
Moffat, Robert, 89
Moltmann, Jürgen, 108
Moozumdar, P. C., 36n.8, 66
Morgan, Robert, 127
Mosala, Itumeleng, 19
Moule, Bishop, 77
muscular Christianity, 61–66
Musopole, A. C., 105

Nandy, Ashis, 126
Narasimhaiah, C. D., 124
Narayan, Kirin, 134
National Christian Council of India, 130
nationalism, 108, 135–39
nativism, 12–14, 132–33
Navalar, Arumuga, 81
Neill, Stephen, 56, 57, 127
Ngugi wa Thiong'o, 94

Orientalism
  background of term, xi
  compared with Anglicism, 9
  contribution of, 134
  current modes of biblical interpretation and, 4–8
  ethnonationalism and, 108–10
  of native scholars, 107–8, 131
  Said's definition of, 102
  third world biblical scholars and, 106–7

translation and, 87–88
of Western biblical scholars,
102–6, 128
Osiek, Carolyn, 106
Other, the
essentializing, 70
Eurocentric perceptions of, 103–4
imperialist argumentation
regarding, 46
the Indian Church Commentaries'
use of, to validate Christian
superiority, 61
postcolonialism as about, 16
translation and the representation
of, 88–89
the West shaping its identity in
relation to, 101–2

Pakenham-Walsh, H., 64, 65, 70, 72
Palakeel, Thomas, 96
Pals, Daniel, 57
Paniker, Ayyappa, 91, 92
Panini, 131
Paranjape, Makarand, 109
Parekh, Bhikhu, 90
philology, 56
Pieris, Aloysius, 128
poor, the, 22–23, 65
postcolonialism
discussion of term, ix–x
elements of a hermeneutics based
in, 15–24
status of topic among exegetes, ix
translation and, 92–97
view of invader/invadee relation,
51
postmodernism, 15
Prakash, Gyan, 16
Pratt, Mary Louise, 51, 52
Precepts (Rammohun Roy), 33–35,
52

Qur'an, the, 63

racism, 88–89
Radhakrishnan, Sarvepalli, 91
Raj, Jaswant, 14

Ramanuja, 73
Ramayana, the, 13
Rammohun Roy, Raja, 66
arguments deployed against
Marshman, 45–50
exegetical principles of, 41–45
hermeneutics of, 35–41
implications of his dispute with
Marshman, 50–52
pruning Gospels to one version, x
sketch of life and work of, 29–33
summary of his *Precepts,* 33–35
rasa method, the, 6–7, 131
Reimarus, H. S., 36n.8, 37
religionism, 93
Renan, Ernest, 36n.8
Rig Veda, the, 73
Robertson, Roland, 138
Roman Empire, the, 68, 75–76
Rowland, Christopher, 104–5
Roy, Arundhati, 94
Rushdie, Salman, 94–95, 96, 134,
137, 139

Sahi, Jyoti, 7
Said, Edward, 54
on culture and imperialism,
125–26
on European scholars' view of the
Near Orient, 113
on Orientalism, xi, 112, 131
on the Orient helping to define
Europe, 61
Western biblical scholars and, 128
on the West shaping its identity
in relation to the Other, 101–2,
104
Sanders, E. P., 113, 118–19
Sankara, 73
Sanskrit
modes of biblical interpretation
based on, 7
nativist challenge to, 12, 13, 132,
134
Orientalists' elevation of, 4, 5, 6,
8, 87, 108, 130–31

Sanskrit (*continued*)
  Rammohun Roy on, 38
  vernacular translations from,
      91–92
Saro-wiwa, Ken, 95
Satchidanandan, K., 95
Sathiasatchy, P. A., 12
Schmid, Deocar, 44–45, 45n.10
Scott, Paul, 84
Semler, J. S., 37
Serampore Baptists, 35–41
Seth, Vikram, 94
Sherwood, Martha Mary, 123–24
Sikhism, 61
Singh, Sadhu Sundar, 13, 132
Soares-Prabhu, George, 23–24,
    93–94
Sobrino, Jon, 106
Song, C. S., 128
Spivak, Gayatri Chakravorty, 129
Stanton, Weitbrecht, 57, 58, 60, 62,
    63, 65, 66, 67, 77
Strauss, D. F., 33, 36n.8
Strecker, George, 126

Tagore, Rabindranath, 73, 130, 138
Tamil, 12, 13, 91–92, 118n.3,
    132–33
Thangaraj, Thomas M., 13
Tharoor, Shashi, 52
Third World: term discussed, xii
Thoburn, Stanley, 10
Thomas, M. M., 128, 136
Thundy, Zacharias P., 115, 116
Tilak, Vaman, 13, 126, 132
totalism, 71
transculturation, 51, 52
translation
  economic and racial
      underpinnings of, 87–90
  effects of, on the colonized,
      90–92
  presupposition of imperial, 86–87
  proposal for a postcolonial
      strategy of, 92–97

Trevelyan, Charles, 8
Trivedi, Harish, 95–96
Tukaram, 73
Tytler, R., 44

untouchables. *See* dalits
Upanishads, the, 107

Valmiki, 91–92
Vandana, Sister, 6, 131
Vedanayagam Sastriar, G. S., 13
Vedas, the, 5, 49–50, 107
Vermes, Geza, 113
vernacular traditions, 8, 12–14,
    91–92, 108, 132–33, 134
Vivekananda, Swami, 36n.8, 117
*Voices from the Margin: Interpreting
    the Bible in the Third World*
    (Sugirtharajah, ed.), 104–5

Walker, T., 56
  on applying exegesis to India,
      57–58
  comparing Roman and British
      Empires, 75–76
  contrasting English and Indians,
      79
  contrasting Hinduism and
      Christianity, 62, 66
  essentialism of, regarding India,
      70
  inculcating the value of humility,
      78
  on Indian women, 74
  totalism of, regarding India, 71
  using military images, 77
  viewing Jesus as an English snob,
      67
Waller, E. H. M., 64–65, 77–78
Ward, William, 87, 88, 89
Westcott, B. F., 55n.3, 55–56, 56n.4
Wickremesinghe, Lakshman, 6, 7
women, Indian, 74–75, 83
Wright, G. Ernest, 80
Wright, Tom, 127

Yates, William, 45n.10